Jesse Halsey.

THE REBIRTH OF RUSSIA

ALEXANDER KERENSKY
Minister of War
"The Lloyd George of Russia"

THE REBIRTH OF RUSSIA

BY

ISAAC F. MARCOSSON

AUTHOR OF "THE WAR AFTER THE WAR,"
"LEONARD WOOD: PROPHET OF PREPAREDNESS,"
CO-AUTHOR OF "CHARLES FROHMAN, MANAGER AND MAN,"
ETC.

"Bind not our souls in bureaucratic chains;
This is now Europe's spring-time; Russia is free,
French fields revive and the defilers flee
Sty-ward driv'n back and drop their long-held gains
Acre by acre—may the April rains
Purge them at last of that impurity,
And make the earth as scarless as the sea !
This is the revolution March ordains,
Rousing our hearts, waking new hopes with stir
Of liberated pinions . . . ."

NEW YORK: JOHN LANE COMPANY
LONDON: JOHN LANE, THE BODLEY HEAD
TORONTO: S. B. GUNDY ∴ ∴ MCMXVII

Press of
J. J. Little & Ives Co.
New York, U. S. A.

TO
HUGH WALPOLE
IN GRATEFUL REMEMBRANCE
OF PETROGRAD DAYS

FOREWORD

THIS little book has no serious historic pretensions. It is frankly journalistic—the record of momentous events chronicled hot on the heel of happening. It was my good fortune to be among the first to reach Petrograd after the Great Upheaval. I found the capital delirious with freedom—the people still blinking in the light of the sudden deliverance. I saw the fruits and the follies of the new liberty.

Whatever social and economic excesses impeded the era of reconstruction—and no one can deny that the path of the infant republic is beset with peril—the larger fact obtains that the Russian Revolution of 1917 set up a distinct milepost in all human progress. If the war which has reddened Europe has achieved no other result, it would have been worth its dreadful cost in blood and treasure. The liberation of the Slav has changed the trend of universal thought, and will affect and underlie the coming centuries. It wrote on the walls of the world the solemn warning that Autocracy's day was done

I. F. M.

New York: July 1917.

CONTENTS

LIST OF ILLUSTRATIONS

The new Russian Democracy
greets the great Republic
of the United States and hopes
to concur with them in the
foundation of a new world on
enlarged international basis of
law and freedom and good will
of Nations

      Paul Milyukoff.

PAUL MILYUKOFF'S MESSAGE TO THE UNITED STATES

PRELUDE

IT was March in London and I was fresh from the battlefields of France. The rumble of great guns boomed in my ears: before my vision still swept the ceaseless panorama of marching troops, rushing munition convoys—the whole dread and distorted picture of a world at war.

I opened my *Times* and something animate seemed to fly out of its pages. I read: "Revolution in Russia: Abdication of the Czar." For three days the cables from Petrograd had been dumb. Here was the reason for the great silence. Now, out of that silence, came the news of a Vast Deliverance. Russia was free!

I had just planned to return to the British armies in France. Here was something bigger, more vital; of immense significance to the whole human race, and especially to the Great Cause for which those armies and all their allies were battling.

But how to get to Petrograd was the problem. All passenger traffic to Norway had ceased since Germany's edict of ruthless submarine warfare had laid its pall of terror upon the Seven Seas. But the British Navy got me started.

Thus it came about that on a brilliant, sunlit morning not many days after, I stood on the deck of a little grey ship that crept out of a land-locked harbour "somewhere in Scotland," and plunged into the barred zone that had become the graveyard of neutral and belligerent shipping. No less treacherous than the foe that lurked beneath its bosom was the North Sea that rose up in its wrath against our mission. A gale blew and gigantic waves almost hid the gallant little destroyers that rode about us.

At evening the wind abated, sunlight flooded the unquiet waters and suddenly before us was revealed, in a majesty unspeakable, the thrilling symbol of Britain's might. It was the Grand Fleet outlined against the fast-ebbing crimson of a wondrous winter sky. Grim, black, unyielding—literally like bulldogs tugging at the leash—these monsters rode the deep.

I have seen many stirring sights in this war but never in all my adventuring have I beheld such inspiring and unforgettable evidence of a nation's authority. The Glory of Empire was incarnated in that bulwark of bristling steel.

The tumult and the terror of angry seas subsided and then came sanctuary amid the Norwegian fjords. Land was never so welcome—and such a land!

Great mountains capped with snow, with all their suggestion of strength and purpose, and at their feet the serene and inland seas. Here was neutral country after months amid the war-ridden regions. Strange sight it was to see a people aloof from stress: stranger was the sound of German and the unfamiliar flash of enemy flags from ship and shop.

I sped by rail through Scandinavia. The brooding crags, the tidy villages, the sight of holiday-seekers at their winter sports—all seemed in strange contrast with the carnage and confusion that I had left behind.

At the Finnish border came the first hint of the Revolution. The red flag was everywhere: soldiers wore crimson rosettes on their breasts: the Marseillaise smote the ear. I pushed on and began the long weary trip through Finland and then at last I crossed the Russian frontier.

We were hours late. The long rattling train stopped. There was the usual collection of passports: the invariable vigil in the carriages behind locked doors and final escape from the heat and stuffiness of the cars into more stuffiness and discomfort in the long Customs Station that reeked with soldiers.

Democracy stood disclosed! Private and captain fraternised arm in arm. The old half-hunted look that had agonised the Russian face of other days was gone. In its stead you saw eager smiles—the animation of a race released from restraint.

I heard my name called, and I walked forward for the usual Customs inquisition and another stamp on the fast-dwindling vacant space on my passport. I found myself before a desk at which sat a superb looking Cossack officer, his breast ablaze with decorations.

He looked up. Quick as a flash he arose and stood at attention. In faultless English he said:

"I am glad to welcome our newest Ally."

"What do you mean?" I asked.

"Your country went to war this morning," he replied.

I had been exiled from news for days. Suddenly I caught up with the march of events and in this dramatic fashion.

Thus it happened that in a dreary Customs shed that seemed a thousand miles from anywhere, and with the cold dawn showing the bleak and snowy landscape outside, came the kindling revelation that America had joined the fight for freedom. It invested Russia with a curious glamour and it gave the war itself a sense of comradeship.

I entered the newest democracy with a kinship in its ideals: a feeling of fraternity with its great desires. The Russian Revolution had almost become a personal thing before I touched it.

ONE morning in March, 1917, the
world read at its breakfast table
that Russia was in Revolution, that
the Czar had abdicated, and that
democracy had arisen out of the ruins of an
ancient imperialism. Nothing that had happened since Prussianism ran amuck was so
fraught with significance for all civilisation.
It affected the whole conduct of the war,
and it will underlie the coming centuries.

Although it broke with startling sudden-
ness, like a bolt of light out of the troubled
sky, it was not a surprise. It was daybreak
after the black night that had long brooded
over Russia. One of the most democratic of
peoples had come into their own.

In the average Anglo-Saxon mind, every
Russian is a revolutionist at heart. Thanks
to the playwright and the novelist, he is pic-
tured as a fierce and bearded Nihilist, foiled
in a bomb-plot and hurried off to Siberia to
become a link in an endless chain of living
tragedy. But there was more truth than

17

imagination in this picture because the story of modern Russia has been a continuous narrative of punitive protest studded with failure and disappointment. The Slav soul was an unuttered aspiration that yearned for fulfilment.

Whatever causes contributed to the Revolution—and they pile up an indictment against misgovernment without parallel—it represents the curious paradox of being both premeditated and accidental. It was premeditated in the fact that since the collapse of the Czar's promise of a real Constitution in 1905 the unrest had mounted steadily: accidental because the brazen attempt to madden the people into unsuccessful revolt that they might be crushed forever gave the unexpected opportunity to rise and be free.

The definite and organised assault on the established order in 1905, brought about by the extreme reactionary policy of von Pleve and the stupidities and the shortcomings revealed in the war against Japan, failed in its real purpose. The Constitution, wrested from the unwilling powers that were, proved to be a hollow mockery: the Duma, held out

as a conciliatory bait in response to a nation-
wide demand for popular government, never
got beyond a debating society. Besides, the
country was at peace and the professional
army remained loyal to its masters.

But the accidental outburst of 1917 succeeded because the Empire was at war and
the nation was armed. The unprofessional
army—that horde in grey that reaction had
called to the colours—would not turn upon
its kind. When this happened the millen-
nium was at hand. It explains the whole
transition from dim despair to realised ideal.
Thus War, the Supreme Revealer, brought
compensation for the ravage that it had
wrought.

The prelude to the awakening was as
sinister as the shadow that had hovered so
tenaciously over Russia. It was streaked
with intrigue, reeked with plot. Borgia
would have blushed at it.

The Revolution was achieved with a
swiftness that startled. The wildest dream
of Russian Liberation only comprehended
a constitutional monarchy. Instead, the
nation was rid of its ruler almost before the
populace knew it, and they got a republic

into the bargain. There is an element of grim humour in the surprise party staged by the Government which turned an intended farce into a stupendous drama of deliverance. It is without precedent in all history.

When the war broke, the country was knit for the moment by common kinship in which all internal grievance and dissension were momentarily forgotten. The bureaucrats at once took fright. In this unity they saw the weapon that would eventually strike at the system by which they thrived. Nothing mattered but their own selfish ends, so now began the reign of graft and treachery that found its first expression in the shameful throttling of military effort, which made the campaigns in the field a series of costly failures. But the blood shed so wantonly rose up in time to confute and to destroy.

The Court and the reactionaries were frankly and almost openly pro-German. How was this possible in a country pledged to the Allied Cause and with immense armies in action against the Central Powers? You did not have to search long for the answer. The Empress who dominated the royal circle was Teutonic to the core; the structure of the bureaucracy owed its existence to the precise prototype of Prussianism. In other words, the evil forces had to stand or fall together. What was a little thing like national honour between despots?

A separate peace with Germany was the end desired. It could be achieved in two ways. One might be dictated by crushing defeats at the front. The other—and apparently it seemed easier—lay through the instrumentality of an uprising at home. The bureaucracy knew that, if civil war could be stirred up, a breach of faith with the Allies, on the grounds of self-preservation, was not only logical, but possible. This nefarious peace would consolidate the evil and autocratic German and Russian systems. In union there was strength. Here then was the ghastly goal toward which the compass of conspiracy was set.

It is not necessary to rehearse in detail here the events by which the country was debased and debauched: how Sukhomlinoff while Minister of War sold the secrets that brought on the Galician reverses: how Sturmer, an avowed German, raised to the Premiership, became paid custodian of the

Kaiser's interests and served them well:
how, when outraged public opinion, born of
shameful exposure of their abuse of office,
forced the arrest of one and the retirement
of the other, they were succeeded by proved
traitors, chief of whom was the unspeakable
Protopopoff—Arch-Protagonist of Liberty,
who, as Minister of the Interior, had the
most powerful post in the Government.

In Protopopoff was incarnated every evil
to which the proverbial Russian official of
story and play was heir. He was both Rod
and Regulator; he ruled by stealth and suppression. He not only recreated the hated
secret police: he *was* the police and likewise
the censorship. He developed his forces
until he had a dread army within the gates
that would do any bidding. He established
an espionage at which the Middle Ages
would have rebelled.

Meanwhile the Monk Rasputin—cruel,
sensual, crafty—had become a Minister
without Portfolio, preying upon the fear and
superstition of courtier and commoner alike
and wielding a fearsome and terrifying authority. With a strange power that was
partly physical and partly hypnotic, he

THE MONK RASPUTIN

swayed the highest circles, made and un-made men until his very name spelled ter-ror. His unholy and unofficial sovereignty gave the situation a touch of mediæval mystery and malignity.

The long-smouldering feelings of the Empire flared out in November, 1916, at the opening of the Duma which had been delayed as long as possible by the Government. The example of France and England in re-making their Cabinets at this time gave the movement for reform an additional impulse, and it was voiced in no uncertain terms. The courageous exposure made by Milyukoff in his famous Duma speech, when he gave concrete evidence of pro-German plots, Ministerial infamy and corruption, and laid bare the dread influence exerted by the Dark Forces, stirred the whole country and not only brought the majority of the upper-middle classes, but some of the nobility and clergy into line with the populace. When Sturmer was removed it seemed that the popular will had at last become effective. Hope kindled in the heart of Russia. Henceforth the Government was practically deserted by everybody except the extreme reactionaries and the pro-Germans. The accession of Trepoff to the Premiership gave additional courage and matters improved, but when he was quickly succeeded by Golitisin, tarred with the reactionary feather, it at once became clear that bureaucracy had come back and was prepared to make a desperate stand for its prerogative and its privilege.

This bureaucracy was in reality a small group of men led in the Ministry by Protopopoff, in the Council of the Empire by Scheglovitoff, who was dismissed from Ministerial office at the same time as Sukhomlinoff, in the Duma by Markoff II., in the church by Pitirim, the Metropolitan of Petrograd, and at the Court by the Empress and Rasputin. Here then were the vultures that gnawed at the very vitals of Russian national life.

In every right-thinking Russian's mind glowed the ideal of a Constitution, and this ideal became more intense as the war unfolded its tragedies. The army was hampered by criminal inadequacy and incompetency. Munitions sent to Russia by her Allies failed to reach the Front, either through studied carelessness or deliberate misappropriation. War appropriations never got beyond the pockets of the plotters who throttled all military effort.

The disorganisation arising from insufficient railway facilities was increased by the division of transport into civil and military spheres. In this way neither the army nor the civil population could be properly served. Immense stores of supplies piled up at Archangel and Vladivostock and could not be moved despite the hunger for them on the battle lines. Yet there was never a dearth of freight cars for a Grand Duke who wanted to ship fertiliser to his estates or haul his crops to the market where he garnered an illicit profit.

To combat this disorganisation public-spirited agencies like the Unions of the Towns and of the Zemstvos and the War Industry Committee did valuable service. The spirit that galvanised these organisations was the spirit that later fed the fires of revolt. Their importance and influence daily became greater and so aroused the alarm of the Government that it did all in its power to hinder their work. During his

term of office Sturmer introduced a number
of regulations placing obstacles in their
way, and on his retirement Protopopoff
continued the same policy. In December,
1916, he forbade the general congress of
these Unions in Moscow on the ground of
their infringing on work which should be
done by the Government. Another measure
aimed directly at this altruistic work was a
law giving the police the right of being
present at all private meetings of any organisation.

The police force throughout the Empire
was strengthened by every possible means
that repression knew. Protopopoff armed
his men with rifles and machine guns intended for the army. He now devoted himself almost exclusively to the development
of the police and press censorship. This
censorship, which had always been rigor-
ous, now became well-nigh intolerable. Although not permitted by law, all the Duma's speeches were censored, and in January, 1917, the press was warned not to re-
fer to the Government except in the most
favourable terms. It became evident that
the Government was using the war while it

lasted to strengthen its hands at the expense of civil liberty.

In the army disaffection was rampant. Up to the beginning of the year that was to change the face of Russia, there had been more than a million intermittent desertions. When men were asked why they came home from the Front in such droves, they shrugged their shoulders and said, "Why stay and fight when there is nothing to fight with?" The vast reserves needlessly called out in 1916 were not kept for the support of the armies in the field but were maintained nearer the Capital, where they could be used in case of uprising.

Seventy per cent. of the munition blast furnaces were idle because of fuel shortage; the metal output (mostly shells) had decreased 75 per cent. No national effort was encouraged to provide the Army and Navy with shells and equipment as was the case in France and England. The Army had only two days' food supply at a time instead of three weeks'. The removal of the Grand Duke Nicholas had a depressing effect because he was implicitly trusted, and this unwavering trust was never bestowed upon the Emperor because of the known German sympathies of his wife.

Matters grew steadily worse. The Court and bureaucratic liaison with Germany continued. The Emperor fluttered about the fringe of affairs—an Imperial figurehead of a husband. When a particularly despicable project was launched he was sent off to the Front like a child in the way of his elders. Sadly the country began to realise that the Government was influenced by only two motives: Pro-Germanism and Self-interest. Russia was beset by an enemy on the border and a more deadly foe at home.

Added to all this was an acute food and fuel crisis. All through an exceptionally severe winter people had been compelled to wait in line in the snow for bread. By the beginning of March the supply in Petrograd began to fail. The scarcity was not due to any lack of supplies. There was ample wheat in the South of Russia, but the chronic failure of the Government to provide railway equipment prevented it from being brought to the Capital. The greed of private contractors, who through bribery were enabled by officials to hold up stores of food until they reached prohibitive prices, was merely one factor in a crisis that was rapidly becoming unbearable. In some cases these contractors permitted perishable food-stuffs to decay rather than lower the price. Then, too, the police became partners in the food cabal, and secreted large quantities of flour in the stations waiting for favourable times to dispose of it at large profits.

In order to fool the people even further and give an impression of food abundance the Government sent long wagon trains of supplies through the streets of Petrograd, but ordered them out again before they could be emptied at the shops. Absurd as this deception seems, it was practised more than once.

The bitter winter of discontent dragged on. Long queues of people shivered for hours in front of the food shops waiting for their dole of bread. But even this hardship did not shake their patience. They consoled each other that it was merely part of the war sacrifice. The Russian is a long-suffering soul.

But there were worse things than the frigid food vigils. Husbands, brothers, and sons were being wasted at the Front that the vampires at home might fatten. A slow anger began to rise. It was heightened by the sight of Sukhomlinoff released from custody; of Sturmer unrepentant and unpunished, of all reaction flaunting its pride and its profit into the face of a distracted and depressed nation. It was intolerable.

Then came the first blow. One morning, not long after our Christmas, Petrograd woke up to find that Rasputin had been killed. Despite the censorship, the glad news trickled through. One of the darkest of the dark forces had been removed, not by plebeian hand, but through aristocratic plot. It was hatched by a Grand Duke and executed by an officer of a high social standing. By means of women—Rasputin's great weakness—he was lured to a private house and then handed a revolver.

"The time has come for you to die," said one of the aristocrats.

The monk seized the weapon and fired a shot wildly through the window. He was immediately riddled with bullets and his body was flung into the Neva. When the policemen, who heard the shots, made inquiry as to what was going on, a member of the murder party replied, and not without truth: "A troublesome dog has been killed."

Though they did not realise it at the time, with that murder the people reached a milepost on their unconscious journey towards the dawn. But the killing was not to go unrebuked.

"I'll cover Russia with scaffolds," said the Czar when he heard of it.

"Watch out that one of them is not yours," replied a courtier more frank than discreet.

The royal revenge began. Rasputin was dead, but the order that he represented still lived, and it set about to strengthen its hold. Protopopoff was charged with the task of administering the lesson on the populace which had begun to take heart again. That silent anger over public and private wrongs was not to be trifled with. The bureaucrats knew that a successful revolution at this time would disrupt the underground railway between Potsdam and Petrograd and endanger the separate peace they so greatly desired. The people were ripe for revolt.

Now was the time to provoke uprising and then overwhelm it so that it would never lift its head again.

Although the people were revolt-ripe, few had any idea that a successful revolution could be undertaken. They realised that any such attempt would only increase their disorganisation and really be capitalised by the enemy. For one thing, they feared that the army would remain loyal to the Emperor, and besides, the immense reinforcements of police everywhere had to be reckoned with. They received the news of the postponement of the Duma in January with calmness, and this seeming supineness now emboldened the Government to direct provocation. Their diabolical task seemed almost too easy.

Conditions favoured the conspirators. The Duma was about to be convened and socialistic protests were likely. These might be construed as the seeds of revolt, so every preparation was made for emergencies. Protopopoff, in anticipation of trouble, concealed machine guns (sent from England, by the way, and intended for the forces in the field) at all commanding positions in the

When they smashed the first window they unwittingly struck the first blow for their liberties. They did not know (and this fact makes the Revolution so remarkable) that they had loosed the whirlwind. All they knew was that they were hungry and cold and determined to get the wherewithal to live.

The desire to eat which had fanned the flame of the French Revolution into a consuming fury, again became the relentless medium which now changed the conspiracy of class into a conquest by the mass.

A Juggernaut which was to crush democracy was converted into the Chariot of Freedom.

city, where they could sweep the streets;
he sent "Black Hundred" agitators into
the factories to stir up strikes and
waited. It was a beautiful scheme, but the
people did not fall for it. The Duma convened without disorder. The workmen remained at their lathes. The great mass of
the people suffered and shivered in the
bread lines and took refuge behind their im-
memorial patience.

Now developed the last desperate attempt
at provocation. Through police and other
agencies (as revelations during and after
the Revolution proved), Protopopoff hoard-
ed and diverted the food and fuel supplies
until there was an actual shortage. What
covert intimidation had started, famine
would now render complete. Yet he did not
reckon with the extent to which hunger will
drive. The slender stores in the shops were
soon exhausted, and there was a new finale
to the long and chilling wait in the bread-
line. It was the empty hand and the emp-
tier stomach.

Then it was that men and women, pang-
driven and weary with fruitless waiting,
went forth, not to doom, but to destiny.

II—*The Great Awakening*

I T was on Thursday, March 8—a date
unique in the annals of freedom—that
these scattered demonstrations began.
Although hunger and discontent
stirred the great mass of the people, there
was no outward or violent manifestation of
the anger that was soon to find expression
in history-making fashion. The first evidence that the Government had taken notice
of the food protest was the galloping of
small companies of Cossacks at full speed
down the Nevsky Prospect, the principal
thoroughfare of Petrograd. They came
and went so swiftly, however, that their
passage only caused momentary gossip.
The general impression among the people
was that industrial trouble had started in
the factories across the river.

In view of what developed, it is interest-
ing, perhaps, to get some mental picture of
what was happening in this city of the Czar
that memorable March day. For the moment Petrograd seemed to be a quiet back-

water aloof from the sanguinary whirlpool
of the Great War. There had been practically no news from the Russian Fronts for
some time, and the new successes of the
British and French on the Western Front
had not aroused any particular enthusiasm.
Save among the incendiary workmen, who
plotted in the dark, there was little or no
talk of Revolution. The very fact that the
opening of the Duma a short time before
had been accomplished so quietly was one
d finite reason why the average person had
no thought of uprising.

By a curious piece of irony, the Duma at
that very hour was occupying itself with a
solemn and stupid debate on the question of
food supplies. The Minister of Agriculture, Rittich, was defending his measures,
and with glib platitudes was assuring the
great mass of the people that they were
needlessly alarmed, and that, before many
weeks would pass, the stomach would be
satisfied. This sort of amiable reassurance
had done its work before, and there seemed
no reason why it should not continue to
appease and satisfy.

The so-called "Intelligentia" of Petro-

CROWD OUTSIDE THE DUMA ON THE FIRST DAY
OF THE REVOLUTION

grad, which, for the want of a better definition, might be termed the educated classes, was somewhat agitated over the recent premier at the Alexander Theatre of an elaborate revival of Lermontov's "Masquerade"—a production that had been five years in preparation, and made on a scale of splendour and extravagance that was in sharp contrast with the spectacle of a distracted nation. As the audiences came and went from this and other theatres, their cabs had frequently to break through the long and shivering lines of people waiting in apparently endless streams before the food bazaars.

But that lane of shivering and waiting humanity had its inevitable turning. When these men and women who had suffered in the icy blasts for hours found the supplies exhausted and their ordeal vain, a snarl of bitter disappointment went up. A dozen shops were stormed, and what little food was found was distributed among the people. The shopkeepers always kept a reserve stock. The outstanding fact to be kept in mind in connection with this most informal outbreak is that it was done without fury or fighting. There was no other disorder.

The next morning it was very evident that a spirit of unrest was abroad. It was not the long dull irritation over continuous abuse of all public patience; it was a definite something, electric with an unseen fire, that boded no good. A number of the daily newspapers and particularly the *Bourse Gazette* and the *Russkaya Volya,* did not appear. It was an ominous sign—a significant silence.

Yet the newspapers that did appear, whether by accident or design, made protest against the existing conditions. The *Retch,* of which Milyukoff was a contributing editor, spoke fearlessly in the following strain:—

"The country must be organised and the population made to feel that everything will be done to relieve the critical position which has arisen. If only the population can be given this assurance we shall see a different picture at once. But without this all efforts will fail, and uncertainty and even worse will grow like a snowball."

Something more deadly than a snowball

was piling up in Petrograd. As the day developed strikes started in many of the factories. But they were not the strikes instigated by the professional agitators of the Government. They grew out of the efforts of revolutionary workmen who realised that the hideous ordeal of having to stand all night in a bread line and then go to work the next morning with an empty stomach must end.

The cry for food became a dull roar. Vast crowds began to assemble on the Nevsky. They were in the main students and workmen whose exterior betrayed no violent intent. But in their eyes was a fixed purpose. The throng included many women and children, largely impelled by that curiosity which is such a strong Russian characteristic.

Suddenly the Cossacks appeared, and the multitude groaned. Here at last were the tools of the despised authority—the relentless force that had trampled every other uprising under foot. Then came the first of the many miracles that were to bewilder Petrograd in the stirring days to come.

Instead of charging the assembly, these

fierce and bearded soldiers rode carefully
among the people. The crowd, in turn,
made way and cheered them as they went.
"Tovarishchi" (comrades), yelled the multitude, and the glad word came echoing back
from the men on horseback. The monsters
smiled—they had become human. It was
incredible but true. Their cruel whips, that
had been the scourge of other days, hung
idly from their saddle-bows. The students
mingled fearlessly with the one-time oppressors who assured them that they would not
shoot even if their officers commanded them.
By nightfall the packed streets buzzed with
the revelation.

Violent hostility was shown towards the
police, however, and some stones and bot-
tles were hurled at them near the Kazan
Cathedral, the most prominent building
on the Nevsky Prospect. During the afternoon an event of utmost significance
occurred. Four workmen were arrested
and concealed in one of the numerous
courtyards in a street that led off the
Nevsky. The hostile crowd immediately
rushed in to rescue them. A group of soldiers stationed in the courtyard had already

raised their rifles to fire, when a band of Cossacks rode up, rescued the workmen and delivered them to the crowd.

There was still no sign of Revolution. It was evident that the great mass of the people were waiting to see what would happen. The only open hostility so far had been directed at the police.

Encouraged by the friendliness of the Cossacks the workmen now went to lengths they had never before attempted. The kerbstone orator broke loose in every direction, and he had eager and willing audiences. One of these men addressed a crowd in the middle of the Nevsky, saying, "We must get rid of the Sturmers and the Golitisins and the Protopopoffs. The people need bread, they cannot work without it."

He was interrupted with several cries of "Down with the War," whereupon he replied: "No, the War must go on. Remember the blood of our brothers and sons must not be spilt for nothing. The thing to do is to get rid of the Government."

In these few words he unconsciously laid bare one of the fundamental reasons why the revolution succeeded. It lay in the fact

that a costly human sacrifice had been laid
on the altar of war, and the people were determined that this sacrifice should not be in
vain. The War was another Calvary!

This speech was wildly applauded. It
was observed that while the man spoke a
group of Cossacks rode up and listened with
interest, made no attempt to disperse the
crowd or interrupt the speaker.

Night fell on a city uneasy and unquiet.
Outwardly there was no sign of Revolution,
but under the surface seethed the great
things. Petrograd was a volcano that slum-
bered.

Saturday morning found the streets
again crowded with curious people. But
there was a distinct change in the vague unrest which had lurked in the air the day before. It seemed to be crystallising. The
reason was that all night long there had
been meetings of workmen stung to the limit
of endurance by the lack of food. On Saturday morning thousands refused to return
to work. Self-preservation was the first
duty, so they joined the mobs that swarmed
everywhere.

The casual passer-by could discern a new

CROWD ON THE NEVSKY PROSPECT, PETROGRAD,
DURING THE REVOLUTION

WORKMEN PARADING ON THE NEVSKY PROSPECT

A BURNED POLICE STATION

A WRECKED POLICE STATION

was found that these supposed soldiers were police who had attired themselves in military uniforms, hoping thus to enflame the mind of the populace against the Army. The ruse did not succeed.

The theatres were open, the cinematograph shows were in full blast and crowded, and the city, except for the absence of tramcars, seemed normal. But if you had listened carefully to the conversations of the hundreds of groups that were assembled everywhere, you would have heard the serious talk of protest, the speech that proclaimed impending event. Workmen were holding meetings in scores of halls, while in the Duma there was anxiety and expectation. Petrograd went to an uneasy bed. No one knew what the morrow would bring forth.

That morrow dawned on blue skies and brilliant sunshine and with a touch of spring despite the glistening snow. Nature was stirring, but not more so than those vast forces unconsciously crouched for momentous leap.

Overnight the Government had not been idle. It suddenly realised that the consum-

mation of the plot against the people was near at hand, little dreaming of the colossal surprise that an outraged public patience had in store.

When the citizens returned to the streets that Sunday morning, they found the walls placarded with warnings showing that the Government had decided on the sternest measures. An official proclamation, signed by Khabaloff, the Military Governor of the town, stated that workmen who did not return to work would be sent to the front immediately. People were warned not to assemble in the streets, as the police and military were authorised to disperse them with all the force at their disposal. These notices, of course, went unheeded.

It was at once apparent that the Government had greatly strengthened its forces. Every highway was patrolled, and thousands of troops were on guard. But no Cossacks were to be seen. Their absence was much commented upon. Despite the almost overwhelming military force that surrounded them, it made the people bolder than ever before. They surged into the prohibited area. The police had their or-

ders to clear the thoroughfare, and they did it the only way they knew how—with the bullet. There was no wholesale slaughter, but during the afternoon, and in a dozen places throughout the city, more than two hundred men, women, and children paid with their lives for the curiosity that took them abroad. Although they weltered in blood, they refused to strike back. The people had bitten at the bait set out for their undoing, but not sharply enough to satisfy the baiters. Apparently they could not even be coerced into their downfall.

As dusk crept over the city, more than one heart sank at the realisation that what had seemed an opportunity to rise the day before had gone the way of all other possibilities. It had not even attained the dignity of a Revolution.

But, even as hope ebbed, the situation was cleared by a swift and sensational event. In the Duma, which had remained in awed and apprehensive session, its President, the mighty Rodzianko—man of iron and action—took the initiative. He sent the Czar the following telegram:—

"Situation serious. Anarchy reigns in

the capital. Government is paralysed. Transport, food and fuel supplies are utterly disorganised. General discontent growing. Disorderly firing is going on in the streets. Various companies of soldiers are shooting at each other. It is absolutely necessary to invest some one who enjoys the confidence of the people with powers to form a new Government. No time must be lost. Any delay may be fatal. I pray God that at this hour the responsibility may not fall on the bearer of the Crown."

At the same time Rodzianko sent copies of this telegram to the various Commanders at the front, and asked for their support in his action. At last a man had arisen!

Without waiting for a reply from the Emperor, the Government acted, and in characteristic fashion. It realised that the Duma had to be throttled. The Premier—Golitisin—had a blank form for dissolution for just such an emergency, and he served it. The Duma was dissolved.

Now came Rodzianko's great hour. Shaking the order for dissolution in his ham of a hand, and in a voice that boomed like a bombardment, he said:—

"They have dissolved the Duma, but it will not be dissolved. Stand with me, my colleagues. From this time on, the Duma is the constituted authority of Russia."

He had faced death on many a hard-fought field, but never did he place his life in such open jeopardy as in this moment when he defied the fates. He was not to stand alone. His towering body—a mountain of angry flesh—became the Rock of Revolution. About it gathered the elements that only needed a leader.

From that time until the Provisional Government was established, the ugly yellow and white Duma building, flanked by quiet gardens and where reaction had mocked at freedom, became the Gibraltar of Uprising. In it was born the new Freedom. Before the Sabbath day, which ushered in Russia's Week of Weeks, had ended, Revolution was at last articulate.

All that night Petrograd quivered with agitation, but it produced the two agencies that, with the Duma, brought about the Supreme Decision. One was the army in the city, which, when beset with the question of firing on its own flesh and blood to-

morrow, declared for humanity. The other was the group of revolutionary workmen hitherto planning in secret that emerged with the new day as the Council of Labour.

Here then were the weapons—uncouth and unformed—that were to overthrow the most buttressed of all autocracies before another sun had set.

A S if by magic, Petrograd bloomed like a crimson rose on Monday morning. No one knew how or why, but on all sides flaunted the red flag of Revolution; "The Marseillaise" was on every tongue. The apathy and indecision of Sunday seemed to have vanished with the night. The issue was at hand, the stage was set, and, almost before the people realised it, they were in the midst of delirious and dramatic doings.

Long before nine o'clock, the streets were black with crowds. Petrograd was all curiosity and eagerness to know what would happen. There were troops everywhere, and it was not long before these men in grey revealed the result of the great decision which the stormy discussions of the night before had evoked.

In other outbreaks, the so-called household troops, together with Cossacks, always stood their ground, bulwark of the imperial

hope, slave of the royal command. But things were different now.

The die had been cast and another one of the miracles was about to happen. The Preobrajenskys, finest of the Guards Regiments, and long the chief pride and protection of the Russian monarchy, revolted when ordered to fire on the mob, shot some of its officers, and then marched down the street singing and cheering.

The Volynskys—also of the Guards—sent to coerce mutineers, joined them, and were soon followed by the Pavlovskys. By noon, nearly twenty thousand troops, the flower of the army, had ranged themselves on the side of the multitude.

At first they wandered about like schoolboys broken out of school. They did not loot; there was no drunkenness; they only shouted, cheered, argued. Crowds of workmen joined them, and the disorganised and officerless mass stormed and captured the Arsenal. An immense store of arms and ammunition fell into the hands of the populace, who could now return the fire of the police.

Things now moved with breathless ra-

pidity. Every regiment sent out from barracks to quell the rising flood of revolt only helped to swell it. The whole city was caught in the swirling eddies of bloody battle. The day of reckoning was at hand.

Petrograd seethed with the rage and the activity of a thoroughly roused people. They had weapons in their hands, and, regardless of what might happen afterwards, the old scores would be settled. The support of the Army was as the breath of life to the cause that now grew stronger with every passing hour.

For years the prisons of the city had loomed up like houses of mystery and murder. To the average man they represented the tombs of hope. They became the first targets of popular fury. First of all the Preventive prison was opened, and a number of political as well as criminal prisoners released. An hour later the Kresty prison on the Viborg side in town was opened, and set on fire, but not until every inmate behind its bars had been set free. Thirdly, the Deportation jail was loosed and still another crowd swarmed forth to freedom.

Strange as it seems, there were no actual

leaders. The streets swarmed with what
seemed to be a confused jumble of soldiers
and armed workmen and students. By instinct they turned on their consistent oppressors, the police. Every station-house
was fired, and the detestable records, dos-
siers, and indictments which had so long
suppressed and thwarted the life and liberty
of the people were quashed by flame.

But greatest prize of all was the destruction of the home of the secret political police. This hotbed of reaction and main-
spring of German intrigue had well been
called the devious spider's web into which
every frank and fearless patriot had been
drawn. It was an object of almost fanatical
hatred, and the spectacle of its burned and
blackened hulk was the sign to all Russia
that the people had kindled one great beacon on the hilltop of their fast-dawning
liberty. What the taking of the Bastille
had been to Paris, the destruction of this
Citadel of the Secret Service was to Petrograd. It marked an epoch.

While this funeral pyre of espionage was
still blazing, the fortress of SS. Peter and
Paul was captured after a very slight re-

on the Massachusetts hillside, was destined
to be heard around the world.

Up to this time there had only been an
orderly protest against the gnawing food
shortage—a deficiency which everybody in
Petrograd knew was within the power of
the authorities to remedy. With the shed-
ding of blood the bars of restraint fell. The
people turned blindly on the police (there
was no hatred for Cossack or soldier),
hurled sticks and stones, and erected rude
barricades. The firing began.

But a striking thing happened. When
called upon to shoot, the soldiers aimed at
the ground or in the air. More than one
officer, enraged at the sight, seized a rifle
from a private and got his victim. It was
a small price to pay for a great knowledge.
Hope clutched at the hearts of the people.
With the Army everything was possible.
In that costly moment of sacrifice was born
the idea that perhaps deliverance was near.
Still there was no outward sign of organised revolt.

In the early evening there was sporadic
shooting, and some of the shots seemed to
come from soldiers. Upon investigation it

element in the atmosphere. There was still curiosity, still a friendly attitude towards the Cossacks and the soldiers who had reinforced them. But more than one man asked his neighbour if the time had not come for action, and if it were not a crime to allow the present opportunity for a determined and organised protest to pass.

By Saturday afternoon what amounted practically to a general strike was on in Petrograd. The crowds of students and women that made the Nevsky almost one solid mass of humanity, had been reinforced by hosts of workmen. The cheerfulness and laughter had subsided. On account of the terrific congestion the tramway service had been suspended, and most of the sleighs had stopped. The almost complete lack of transportation facilities gave the city a strange hushed look.

Mounted police now reinforced the Cossacks and troops, and with their advent the clash came. Just off the Nevsky one of them killed a man who refused to be jostled. It was the first shot of the Revolution, and, like the report that rang out that April day

sistance. Here was housed the Royal tomb
and the Mint. Thus even the last resting-
place of the dictators was now swept by the
cool clean breath of freedom.

Still no word came from the Czar. Despite all its elaborate preparation, the Government for the moment seemed helpless in
the face of the raging upheaval. Rodzianko
now sent a second telegram to the Czar
which read:

"Matters becoming worse. Must take
immediate steps or to-morrow may be too
late. The last hour is come in which to decide the fate of the country and the dynasty."

Then for the first time the Emperor
spoke. He wired the Military Governor
of Petrograd that he was sending an army
from the Front to quell the insurrection,
and that he would come in person to be in
at the death of the abortive attempt. It was
the last order that the Little Father was to
give to the people who had been his obe-
dient children. He did not know it, but the
reins of power had for ever passed from his
hands.

Meanwhile the disorganised revolt had
developed into a more or less systematic in-

surrection. The streets and four-fifths of
the city were in complete possession of the
Revolutionists, who now seized hundreds of
motor cars and lorries, manned them with
armed men who tied red rags to their bay-
onet points and raced madly through the
streets. It was a new kind of joy riding.

Now began a man-hunt without precedent. All the troops had come over to the
people; only the detested police remained
to be routed. Protopopoff had cached them
on roofs with abundant supplies of food,
and from these vantage points they sniped.
A shot from the top of a building became
the signal for the doom of every inmate.
Day and night this relentless police pursuit
continued. They were dug out like rats.
In their rage the pursuers often flung their
oppressors into the street, sometimes after
killing them with their naked hands. It is
doubtful if any other great popular upheaval has ever witnessed such bitterness as
was displayed by the people of Petrograd
against the police. The only parallel perhaps may be found in the attitude of the
citizens towards the aristocracy during the
French Revolution.

This ruthless hunt was not without its picturesque detail. A squad from one of the Guards regiments were accosted at the corner of a street by a Boy Scout not more than ten years of age. He held a large Browning pistol in one hand, and with the other grasped an officer's sword. "Come, you men, quickly," he said, "I know where two policemen are hiding." With smiling faces the men followed their little guide into a yard, and were absent about ten minutes. Presently the Scout came out with the utmost satisfaction and leading forth his small company of good-humoured giants with two policemen, in a dishevelled state, in their midst.

Amid this tumult of revenge and revolt were revealed qualities that made the insurrection unique and distinct. Out of the chaos came a crude order, and with it the marshalling of virtues that in such an hour of righteous retribution seemed foreign. It was a liberal education in control. Whatever economic excesses may hamper the period of Russian readjustment, this restraint will always be a badge of honour for the men who rode the whirlwind Revolution.

First of all, and with the unconsciousness which marked so much of the revolutionary effort (it was nothing more than instinct), was the formation of a civilian police. "If our cause must prevail," said Rodzianko, "we must first have order." Students, most of them mere boys, formed the force, and they remained for months the only sign of armed control in Petrograd.

Although many shops were emptied of their stores, they were, in the main, establishments of greedy merchants who had imposed upon the need of the people. A sort of Robin Hood reprisal was vented.

Some troops were fired on by the police from the roof of the Astoria Hotel, where many of the Government officers lived, and where liquor was dispensed in violation of the prohibition law. It was immediately attacked and searched. But, instead of drinking the large stores of wine in the cellars, the soldiers poured it in the gutter.

The absence of vodka proved to be a blessing of the first magnitude, and contributed enormously to the success of the en-

TROOPS AND STUDENTS FIRING ON POLICE STA-
TIONED ON THE HOUSETOPS

MOTORS WERE SEIZED AND MANNED BY TROOPS
AND STUDENTS

terprise. Indeed, in looking back over those
stirring days, it is quite evident that when
the Czar signed the decree for the prohibition of liquor at the beginning of the war
he likewise signed the death-warrant of the
Romanoffs.

During the raid on the Astoria Hotel a
woman offered some soldiers a handful of
money to protect her.

"Keep your money," said a brawny ser-
geant, "we are on a different job now."
Here was the repression that became one
of the marvels of that marvellous hour.

Although every one knew that vast transition was in process, there was no actual
news, for the newspapers had all suspended
publication. On the very first night of the
Revolution, handbills, written and printed
by volunteers, appeared on the streets for
free distribution. They told briefly and
frankly just what was happening. Pub-
licity, the old foe of the crumbling system,
was turned full tilt upon the new order.
The knowledge of what was going on
brought comfort and cheer to those who
stood on the frontiers of the tremendous
events.

The Duma seethed. At this tribunal of the budding nation, Rodzianko and his co-horts kept incessant watch. All roads led to it: it was both camp and court. Regiment after regiment marched in to offer loyalty. The accession of the famous Pre-obrajensky Guards provided a stirring and characteristic incident.

The men and their officers (for all of them were not shot), giants all, were drawn up in ranks, four deep, down the whole length of the huge Catherine Hall. Rod-zianko stepped forth to welcome them. On his appearance, the commanding officer's voice rang out—"Preobrajensky, atten-tion!" and the whole regiment stood at salute.

The President of the Duma then ad-dressed them as follows:—

"I want to thank you for coming here to help the members of the Imperial Duma to establish order and to safeguard the honour and glory of your country. Your comrades are fighting in the trenches for the might and majesty of Russia, and I am proud that my son has been serving since the begin-ning of the war in your gallant ranks.

But, in order that you should be able to advance the cause and interests which have been undertaken by the Duma, you must remain a disciplined force. You know as well as I do that soldiers are helpless without their officers. I ask you to remain faithful to your officers and to have confidence in them, just as we have confidence in them. Return quietly to your barracks and come here at the first call when you may be required."

"We are ready," answered the Preobrajensky Guards. "Show us the way."

"The old authority is incapable of leading Russia in the right way," was the answer. "Our first task is to establish a new authority in which we could all believe and trust, and which would be able to save and magnify our mother Russia."

In the same way, Rodzianko greeted the officers and men of the Grenadier Guards and the troopers of the Household Cavalry.

In one way or another, much effective missionary work was done among the soldiers that day. Milyukoff visited the Barracks of the First Reserve Regiment and addressed the men, while Kerensky visited

Mikhailovsky Artillery College with a similar purpose.

Most of the insurgent troops were quite ready to accept the profession of faith made by the Duma. When one delegation arrived, however, and asked point-blank what the attitude of the assembly was, Rodzianko made the following significant statement:—

"The present critical moment is marked by the passing of the old authority and the coming of the new. In accomplishing this, the Duma is taking an active part, but before everything it is necessary to have order and quiet."

This injunction, it is worth emphasising, was the burden of every utterance that went out from the men in authority during those turbulent days. As a symbol of that order, the Preobrajenskys took up their station in the Duma and became the watch-dogs of the legislative halls.

This revel of Revolution was very fine and stirring, but it could not be maintained without some definite and organised control. The Duma went into executive session, and it was decided to establish a Provisional Government. Before the final vote was taken, however, Rodzianko received an invitation by telephone to attend a meeting of the Council of Ministers at the Marie Palace, where the Council of Empire—the upper body of the Duma— held its sessions.

Rodzianko proceeded thither, safely traversing the entire city under a guard of the Duma troops in armoured cars. He found all the Ministers assembled, and also the Grand Duke Michael, brother of the Czar. Rodzianko informed them that the Duma, acting in accordance with the nation, had decided to constitute a Provisional Government, as they saw no other way of re-establishing order in the capital, of saving the country from anarchy, and of enabling Russia to continue the War to a victorious finish.

The majority, if not all of the Ministers, appeared to be willing to surrender, and seemed disposed to agree to the appointment of the Grand Duke Michael as Regent. But General Beliaeff, Minister of War, declared that it was impossible for him to violate his oath as a soldier, and announced his determination to continue the struggle until he received orders to the contrary from the Czar.

After Rodzianko's return to the Duma, the House unanimously voted the motion creating the Provisional Government. Orders were then given for the arrest of the members of the old Government, but when the representatives of the Duma reached the Marie Palace they found that the birds had flown and were hiding in the Prefect's Palace.

Meanwhile, upwards of a hundred officers had come to offer their services to the Duma, and had been placed in command of battalions and companies which had joined the national cause. Captain Karauloff, a Cossack Deputy, took command of the troops at the Duma, while another Deputy, Colonel Engelhart, a Guardsman, who had discharged important Staff offices during the war, was appointed Commandant of Petrograd.

Rodzianko at once formed what was called the Executive Committee of the Duma, which became the nucleus of a Provisional Government. It included Rodzianko, Prince Lvoff, who had come up from

Moscow to help, Kerensky, the Social Labour Deputy, destined to loom up henceforth
as the dominant man of that kindling hour,
Milyukoff, Nekrassoff, Konavoloff, Mitry-
ukoff, Chiedze, Shulgin, Schidlovski, Karauloff, and Rjevski.

The Committee immediately issued this
proclamation:

"The Provisional Committee of members
of the Imperial Duma finds itself compelled, by the onerous circumstances of internal chaos, resulting in the measures taken
by the old Government, to take in hand the
re-establishment of State and public order.

"Fully appreciating the responsibility it
assumed, the Committee feels confident that
the people and Army will help it in the difficult task of creating a new Government
capable of meeting the wishes of the nation
and deserving its confidence."

This was followed up by a second proclamation urging law and order. It read:

"The Provisional Committee of the Imperial Duma appeals to the inhabitants of
Petrograd, in the common interest, to spare

public and State institutions and services,
such as telegraphs, waterworks, electric
power stations, tramways, and Government
offices. Similarly, it confides to the protection of the citizens all mills and factories
working for munitions or for general re-
quirements. It should be borne in mind
that damage to, or destruction of, institutions cause enormous harm to the Empire
and to the inhabitants, inasmuch as all alike
need water, light, etc.

"Likewise, it is inadmissible that there
should be any harm done to the lives and
property of private persons. The spilling
of blood, and the plundering of property,
will remain a blur on the conscience of the
person resorting to such acts of violence,
and may also cause untold privations to the
inhabitants of the city."

The effect of these proclamations, with
their injunction for restraint and reconstruction, was admirable. While a few soldiers were able to obtain vodka and became
intoxicated (and this vodka, by the way,
had been mobilised by Protopopoff for the
express purpose of inflaming the insurrec-

STUDENTS OF PETROGRAD, LEADERS IN THE REVO-
LUTION

TYPICAL RUSSIAN "TOMMIES"

tion), these excesses were the exception and
not the rule. It cannot be too strongly
stated that, considering the extraordinary
provocation, the behaviour of the average
Russian citizen in these hours of frenzy is
almost without parallel in the whole story
of popular uprising.

The Duma continued to be the Mecca of
all efforts, and, as the day waned, soldiers
and students began to bring in prisoners.
The combing out of reaction yielded a big
bag. But there was no gloating. The triumph was tempered with a rude mercy, for
few of the ancient despoilers resisted.

At midnight a forlorn-looking man in a
fur coat spoke to an armed civilian outside
the Duma.

"Are you an officer?" he asked.

"Yes," was the reply.

"Then take me to the Committee of the
Duma," responded the stranger. "I am
Protopopoff, late Minister of the Interior.
I surrender myself voluntarily."

Well might the people have said, "Vengeance is mine," and taken it relentlessly,
but they merely thrust him into a wing of
the Duma under a guard.

That night the Nevsky was illuminated from end to end by powerful searchlights placed on the Admiralty steeple. These brilliant arrows of light pointed the path of the new day that had come for Russia.

So ended the crowded Monday of March 12. Revolution was no longer in question; it was achieved and the army in Petrograd had made it possible. But what of the armed host which even then might be on its way with the Czar? He was still Emperor in name. Petrograd's dreams that night were gaunt with the fear of bloody civil war.

IV—*The Birth of a Nation*

THE fear of civil war was groundless. Every regiment that trooped into town enrolled under the red flag. Tuesday, the 13th, became Freedom's lucky day.

But the fight of Petrograd was not yet entirely won. The city was still a sporadic battlefield, and the police-hunt continued with unremitting zeal and hatred. The stupid minions of Protopopoff had received their orders to remain at their stations on the roofs and to keep them at any hazard. Most of them kept on firing without having the intelligence to submit to the inevitable, and the result was that thousands were wiped out. The remainder escaped either in civilian clothes or in the uniform of soldiers, which they acquired by methods best known to themselves.

One stronghold of the old Government remained untaken. It was the huge Admiralty building, which stood at one end of the Nevsky. Here, under the direction

69

of General Khabaloff, reaction made its last stand. Field and machine guns were disposed in the huge courtyard, and detachments of troops of all arms took up their stations. The revolutionary soldiers began a siege which continued with hot firing on both sides all day and night.

On Tuesday morning a letter was sent to General Admiral Grigorovitch, the Naval Minister, stating that if the Admiralty was not surrendered within half an hour it would be immediately destroyed by heavy fire from the big guns of the fortress of Peter and Paul. The Minister realised that the destruction of this building would entail the loss of its valuable records, so by arrangement with General Khabaloff, the building was evacuated and the troops surrendered. The latter, however, immediately joined their colleagues and became recruits of the red brotherhood.

On the door of the Admiralty was posted this notice: "Under the protection of the State Duma." This became the seal that was fast hardening on every sign of the tottering régime. The whole of Petrograd was now in the hands of the Revolution.

The Duma remained the storm centre of historic events. It was still a babel of tongues: a litter of food, arms, and impedimenta. Every delegation of troops and workmen brought in some sort of supply. Dispute and controversy raged in a perfect maelstrom. Buffets for feeding the soldiers had suddenly sprung up and every conceivable kind of Committee was named. Could coherency emerge from this blatant confusion? Somehow it did.

The food problem naturally engaged attention at once because hunger could not be appeased by freedom. A Committee on provisions was named, and the vast stores of flour secreted by Protopopoff and the rest of the old Government were seized. Before twenty-four hours had passed, a rude transport of supplies had been established as the result of an earnest appeal telegraphed to towns and villages throughout the country, urging the farmers to bring in their grain and flour and sell them to the agents of the Zemstvos, in order that the armies and the metropolis might be fed.

In Petrograd all the restaurants had been closed for three days, and, by one of the many ironies that marked the Revolution, the wealthier classes were thus unable to obtain food except in those cases where there were ample reserve supplies. The poorer classes fared much better. Once released from the grip of the police, the smaller shopkeepers met the moment with commendable decency. Not being compelled to pay graft to the avaricious middle-man or the still more gold-thirsty police, they at once reduced their prices.

There were many examples of whole-hearted generosity by the ordinary people. One teashop displayed a notice on its window that voiced the feelings of many small merchants. It was ungrammatical, badly spelt and written in an uncouth hand, but it showed the right spirit. Here it is:

"Fellow-citizens! In honour of the great day of freedom I bid you all welcome. Come inside and eat and drink to your heart's content."

The owner of the shop, wearing a red shirt—for red had become the prevailing colour of fashion—himself greeted his guests and distributed food and unlimited quantities of tea.

The bagging of prisoners went on. Sturmer was taken at his lunch table at the English Club—which, by the way, did not have a single English member—and hurried first to the Duma and then across the river to the fortress of Peter and Paul, where he was soon joined by Pitirim, the Metropolitan of the Church, and Kurloff. A few hours later the aged Goremykin, who had so long persisted in remaining in power, blind and deaf to the dictates of the time, was taken. Another arrest of great importance was that of Dubrovin, the infamous leader of the "Black Hundred."

The arrest of the archtraitor Sukhomlinoff created one of the many sensational episodes that crowded thick and fast upon this day of days. He was found in the apartment of a friend and dragged in full uniform to the Duma. The restraint which had marked the taking of most of the oppressors vanished at the sight of the betrayer of his country. There was a rush to rend him. Kerensky heard the uproar,

and, placing himself before the shuddering
and cowering figure, said dramatically:

"Every man in Russia is now to have a
fair trial. I shall be responsible for Sukhomlinoff. If you kill him you must kill
me first."

It was the first enunciation of the new
rule of justice, and it prevailed. Sukhomlinoff was stripped of his eqaulets and led
off to join his colleagues of the perverted
conspiracy in the dungeon of the old fortress, whose guns even then were sounding
the requiem of the monarchical power.

Every hour now brought fresh and
strong addition to the forces of Revolution.
One of the most notable was the famous
command known as the Sailors of the
Guard, under the command of the Grand
Duke Cyril, who came in person, with his
officers, and assured the Duma that the
historic corps would be loyal to the new
order. Addressing Rodzianko, the Grand
Duke said with emotion:

"I have the honour to appear before your
Excellency and to place myself at your disposal. In common with our nation I desire the welfare of Russia. This morning

A BARRICADE DURING THE REVOLUTION

A STREET SCENE DURING THE REVOLUTION

I assembled my men, and explained to them
the significance of present events, and I can
now say that the whole Naval Guard Corps
is at the entire disposal of the Imperial
Duma."

Amid much cheering, Rodzianko said:

"The words of the Grand Duke have
given me much pleasure. I am confident
that the Naval Guards, like all the rest of
our forces, will help us to vanquish our
foe."

Subsequently the whole Corps mustered
at the Duma, and, led by the Grand Duke
and his officers, marched past, saluting
Rodzianko.

The whole General Staff College, num-
bering three hundred and fifty officers,
joined the new Government. All the Cossacks and other units also proclaimed their
allegiance.

As actual battle subsided in the streets a
new conflict arose within the walls of the
Duma. The old Tauris Place now housed
an unrest far more dangerous than all the
confusion that the stirring days had
brought about. A bitter controversy over
the form of Government developed.

During the two days in which the old order was overthrown, the Council of Labour, which had been born with the Revolution, had steadily grown in size and authority. It expressed the bitter class interests of the city, and was the one group that now thought only of itself and its desires in the midst of the Great Awakening. It drew to its ranks various representatives of the Army, and now became the Council of Workmen's and Soldiers' Delegates. This self-constituted assembly, whose members, it must be admitted, had large and significant part in making the Revolution possible, because the first sign of organisation had come from the Labourites, was now in full and flaming swing in the Finance Chamber of the Duma. Every rabid Socialist and Radical had his innings of speech and demanded an unrestrained and social Republic at once.

The great body of sentiment in the Duma, headed by Lvoff, Rodzianko, and Milyukoff, still had the ideal of a Constitutional Government. Cheidze, the Socialist, and Kerensky formed the link between the two bodies. The Labour group insisted upon their very extreme demands. Their power was constantly increased by the arrival of troops from the country, who came at once under the control of the Radicals. Now began the real struggle between the Social Democrats on the one hand and the Executive Committee of the Duma on the other. Each side began to issue manifestos to the people, and a dual government seemed at hand.

The announcements of the Duma were sane, sober, and constructive, in the same key as the first two proclamations of the Executive Committee. The earlier appeals of the Council were inclined to be high and dignified in purpose, as the following proclamation attests:

"To the Soldiers:

"Soldiers! The people of Russia thank you for your revolt in the cause of freedom.

"Eternal memory to those who have fallen!

"Soldiers, some of you still hesitate to join the revolt of your and our comrades.

"Soldiers, remember your weary lives in the villages, in the factories, in the workshops, where the Government suffocated and oppressed you. Join the people, and the people will give you and your families a new and free life and happiness.

"Soldiers, if you are driven from your barracks, go to the Duma—there you will find comrades whose joys and sorrows you will share.

"Soldiers, do not shoot at random in the streets. On the roofs of houses and in private flats the remainder of the police force is hidden, the 'Black Hundred' and other vagabonds. Try and get them out by sharp-shooting or correct attack.

"Soldiers, keep order everywhere. Form companies and take charge of all military matters which concern the defeat of the enemy.

"Soldiers, do not let the hooligans molest peaceful citizens, do not permit shops to be looted, nor private flats—that must not be done.

"For all information and orders, apply to the Duma, where there will always be found the Military Commission of the Town of Petrograd.

"Be firm and unbending in your decision to fight to death for freedom.

"Better death than that the enemy should triumph. Victims, your service and your honour will never be forgotten by Russia. Long live freedom!"

But as the strength of the Council grew, its utterances became bolder—even seditious. The Social Democrats had the upper hand and they set about to democratise the army. A characteristic manifesto, scattered broadcast among the troops, contained these disquieting commands:

"(1) The orders of the Executive Committee must be obeyed, saving only on those occasions when they shall contravene the orders and regulations of the Council of Workmen's and Soldiers' Delegates.

"(2) In private life, standing to attention and compulsory saluting off duty is abolished.

"(3) In like manner is abolished the addressing of officers as 'Your Excellency,' 'Your Honour,' which shall be replaced by the address by 'Gospodin General' (Mr. General).

"(4) Uncivil conduct towards soldiers of all military ranks, and the addressing of them in private by the word 'Thou' is forbidden. In all cases of misunderstanding between officers and soldiers, the latter shall report to the Company Committee."

Here was the first clash with the Executive Committee at the Duma, but more dangerous than this was the injunction which immediately began to disrupt the discipline among the soldiers. The Russian private, always a most willing disciple of restraint, immediately broke loose. He showed an open disrespect for his superiors, at once stopped saluting, and an era of military disorganisation began that promised ill.

While this social strife raged there came forth the first cheering evidence of the New Freedom. The Executive Committee of the Duma issued the following momentous appeal to the people of Russia:

"Citizens:

"The Provisional Executive Committee of the Duma, with the aid and support of the garrison of the capital and its inhabitants, have now triumphed over the noxious forces of the old régime in such a measure as to enable it to proceed to the more stable organisation of the executive power. With this object, the Provisional Committee will name Ministers of the first National Cabinet, men whose past political and public activity assures them the confidence of the country.

"The new Cabinet will adopt the following principles as the bases of its policy:

"I. An immediate amnesty for all political and religious offences, including terrorists' acts, military revolts, and agrarian crimes.

"II. Freedom of speech, of the press, of association and labour organisation, and the freedom to strike, with an extension of these liberties to officials and troops, in so far as military and technical conditions permit.

"III. The abolition of social, religious, and national restrictions.

"IV. Immediate preparations for the summoning of a Constituent Assembly, which, with universal suffrage as a basis, shall establish the Governmental régime and the Constitution of the country.

"V. The substitution for the police of a national militia, with elective heads and subject to the self-government bodies.

"VI. Communal elections to be carried out on the basis of universal suffrage.

"VII. The troops that have taken part in the revolutionary movement shall not be disarmed, but they are not to leave Petrograd.

"VIII. While severe military discipline must be maintained on active service, all restrictions upon soldiers in the enjoyment of social rights granted to other citizens are to be abolished."

Up to this time, the whole action of the Revolution had been confined to Petrograd. It was a world of revolt all its own. No news of these epoch-making happenings had, as yet, reached the outside, because, at the first sign of revolt, the old Government had stopped all telegraphic communication. So far as the rest of the world was concerned, Russia was dumb.

Meanwhile, Moscow had proclaimed itself on the side of the Duma, and all the troops there had come over to the Revolution. The police, acting under instructions of Protopopoff, had placed themselves in readiness for the revolt, but they were soon dug out and sent to the Front, and with very little bloodshed, and the city became normal. Coincident with this reassuring news came communications from Generals Russky and Brusiloff, stating that the armies under their command had accepted the new régime and could be counted on.

Everything seemed too good to be true. The actual Revolution had been achieved with such slight loss and effort that it was like a dream.

That dream was now to be rudely disturbed because the differences between the Duma and the Council of Workmen's and Soldiers' Delegates became acute. The Council renewed its request for a red Republic, and flooded the city with seditious literature. It forgot the War, the uncertainties of the troubled hour, everything except its own selfish demands.

The Duma still persisted in its ideal of a Constitutional Monarchy. Its attitude was best expressed by a cablegram sent the day

before to the Czar by the Reform Group
in the Council of the Empire, which read as
follows:

"The maintenance of this old Government in office is tantamount to the complete
overthrow of law and order, involving defeat on the battlefield, the end of dynasty,
and the greatest misfortunes for Russia.

"We consider that the only means of salvation lies in a complete and final rupture
with the past, the immediate convocation of
Parliament, and the summoning of a person enjoying the confidence of the nation,
who shall form a new Cabinet capable of
governing the country in full accord with
the representatives of the nation."

The issue between Moderates and Extremists became sharply defined, and a Revolution inside a Revolution developed that
threatened the whole new-found deliverance.

Kerensky now stood revealed as the great
Pacificator. Though bound to Radicalism
by every tie of birth and sentiment, his
larger patriotism overcame all else. His
oratory curbed the incendiaries. The Coun-

cil of Workmen's and Soldiers' Delegates withdrew its opposition to the Duma for the moment at least, and the work of reconstruction went on. The proclamation of the Executive Committee enunciating the new order was the result.

The curb on the Radicals was short-lived, and again a heated and acrimonious discussion ensued. Incidental to all the wrangle about the new form of Government was the squabble over the disposition of the Czar. He was like a piece of furniture that had suddenly ceased to be useful or ornamental, and had to be done away with. But how? The Social Democrats shrieked for his life; the Moderates pleaded for the Czarewich. Many failed to remember that Nicholas was still Emperor, and to millions throughout Russia the now despised name remained part of every prayer. He had not shown his hand.

WHILE the Duma rocked with frenzied debate there was written in the quiet of an obscure Russian town one of the supreme chapters in the story of Russian emancipation. It recorded an event that will stand out with epic significance, no matter what other sensations the Great War may produce. It was the Czar's final ordeal, and, like other occasions of far-flung and permanent interest, had a simple, almost humble setting. But the tremendous importance of the hour made it one of the historic spots of all time. In that aloof moment, far from all the glamour and glitter of Royal Court, the Emperor reaped the harvest of the long years of his mistaken rule.

During those stirring days when Petrograd was in revolution, the Czar had been at the Front, sent there because of the near consummation of the plot of the reactionaries to provoke an uprising. That storm, as you have seen, overwhelmed the provoker, but it took several days before it beat about the head of the most spectacular victim of it all.

Nicholas had ignored Rodzianko's first telegram, and this omission cost him his crown. Had he acted wisely and promptly he could not only have firmly re-established himself upon the throne, but in the hearts of his subjects. But the delay, hesitancy, and indecision which had always characterized him now marked him for destruction.

History was repeating itself with Nicholas. On another epochal day in his life— that memorable May the 10th in 1906 when the first Duma assembled—he faced a great opportunity for vital and compelling leadership. But he met it with high-sounding platitudes and empty promises. Then he was surrounded by all the hollow pomp and shallow brilliancy of a time-serving Court; now he stood alone with his destiny, and it spelled the end of power.

When he finally made answer to Rodzianko's second appeal, it was with the announcement that he was sending an army to crush Petrograd, and that he was com-

ing in person to be in at the death of what
seemed to be just one more futile effort for
freedom. He was destined to witness the
failure of that project, for fate had singled
him out for her own, and from that moment
pursued him relentlessly.

The Czar had started back to Tzarskoe
Selo, his palace just outside Petrograd, and
had reached Bologoi, a small station, when
the Imperial train came to a sudden stop.
The tracks ahead had been pulled up by
some revolutionary workmen. It was the
first sign of the larger barrier that an
avenging nation was rearing in his path.
He returned to Pskoff—General Russky's
Headquarters—and there awaited his doom.

The ill tidings—that is, ill for him—had
travelled faster than he. He summoned
General Russky to his presence, and learned
for the first time of the sweep of the revolt.
It dazed and saddened him. He became
silent and retired to his carriage in the
royal train.

At two o'clock the next morning he sent
for General Russky, and, with the manner
of making a great surrender, said to him:

"I have decided to give way and grant

ONE OF THE CZAR'S MOTOR-CARS, SEIZED IN THE IMPERIAL GARAGE, AND
PARADED IN TRIUMPH

my people a responsible Ministry. What is your opinion?"

As a matter of fact the Czar had already written out the manifesto, and it was signed and sealed at the table of the royal compartment.

In that cold grey morning hour he believed sincerely that he was submitting to the popular will. As a matter of fact, he had long since passed the time when he could indulge in condescension.

"If you want my frank opinion, your Majesty," replied General Russky, "your manifesto is too late. I suggest, however, that we get in touch with Rodzianko."

The Czar went back to bed, and General Russky called up Petrograd and conversed for two hours with the President of the Duma. It was probably one of the most momentous conversations that the telephone has ever transmitted. Rodzianko told the General of the chain of events that had converted Petrograd from a police-ridden and cowed community into a free and triumphant municipality. He impressed the fact that the Czar must abdicate; that it was the only chance to save his life.

When Russky returned to the Imperial
train he found his royal master dishevelled
and discouraged. He had not slept a wink.
He at once communicated to him the result
of his conversation with Rodzianko.

"Do my other Generals know of this?"
asked the Emperor still clutching at a last
hope.

"Yes, your Majesty, they not only know,
but concur in the feeling that an abdication
is necessary," was the answer.

"Then send for Rodzianko," commanded
the Czar, and he set about preparing the
form of abdication.

Rodzianko could not leave the helm of the
Duma, so Gutchkoff and Shulgin, a Conservative Deputy, came instead. Their
train was delayed. The long grey winter
afternoon dragged on while the Czar of
all the Russias fretted and pulled nervously
at his moustache. The ruler who had kept
two hundred millions of people waiting now
waited with eager but sad impatience for the
coming of two civilians.

General Russky had left word that the
two representatives of the Duma be brought

to him first, but through some mistake they were taken at once to the royal train.

They found the Emperor in a dimly lit carriage. He was pale, nervous, and care-worn. The real facts of this noteworthy occasion do not disclose an heroic renuncia-tion. Save for one faithful attendant, Count Fredericks, the Czar of all the Russias was alone. He did the only thing that was left for him to do.

"Tell me the truth," he said.

"All the troops in Petrograd are on our side," replied Gutchkoff. "It is useless to send more regiments. They all go over to our side as soon as they reach the city."

"I know it," replied the Czar. After a pause he continued: "What do you want me to do?"

"Your Majesty must abdicate in favour of the Heir Apparent, under the Regency of Grand Duke Michael Alexandrovitch. Such is the will of the new Government we are forming under Prince Lvoff," was Gutch-koff's command.

"I cannot part with my boy," spoke the monarch, with the only emotion that the

scene had evoked. "I shall hand the Throne
to my brother."

He who had been a god-head looked help-
lessly around. Then, speaking in the most
matter-of-fact way, he said:

"Have you a sheet of paper?"

A blank page was produced, and with a
fountain pen, loaned by Gutchkoff, was written the manifesto that signed away the most
complete power that any modern monarch
had known.

The full text of the Magna Charta of the
Russian people was as follows:

"By the Grace of God, We, Nicholas II.,
Emperor of all the Russias, Czar of Poland,
Grand Duke of Finland, etc., to all our faith-
ful subjects be it known:

"In the days of a great struggle against a
foreign enemy, who has been endeavouring
for three years to enslave our country, it
pleased God to send Russia a further painful
trial.

"Internal troubles threatened to have a
fatal effect on the further progress of this
obstinate war. The destinies of Russia, the
honour of her heroic Army, the happiness of

NICHOLAS II.

the people, and the whole future of our beloved country demand that the war should be conducted at all costs to a victorious end.

"The cruel enemy is making his last efforts, and the moment is near when our valiant Army, in concert with our glorious Allies, will finally overthrow the enemy.

"In these decisive days in the life of Russia we have thought that we owed to our people the close union and organisation of all its forces for the realisation of rapid victory; for which reason, in agreement with the Imperial Duma, we have recognised that it is for the good of the country that we should abdicate the Crown of the Russian State and lay down the Supreme Power.

"Not wishing to separate ourselves from our beloved son, we bequeath our heritage to our brother, the Grand Duke Michael Alexandrovitch, with our blessing for the future of the Throne of the Russian State.

"We bequeath it to our brother to govern in full union with the national representatives sitting in the Legislative Institutions, and to take his inviolable oath to them in the name of our well-beloved country.

"We call upon all faithful sons of our native land to fulfil their sacred and patriotic duty in obeying the Czar at the painful moment of national trials and to aid him, together with the representatives of the nation, to conduct the Russian State in the way of prosperity and glory.

"May God help Russia!"

He bowed his head for a few moments, took the pen, and, apparently without a trace of feeling, affixed his signature. When he rose from the chair the Czar of all the Russias had become plain Nicholas Romanoff.

It was indeed the twilight of the imperial gods.

PETROGRAD remained in ignorance of the Czar's abdication for twenty-four hours. The capital was so absorbed in the hectic discussion over the new form of government that for a moment it lost sight of the man who had been the root of all their troubles and who at that moment was passing into eclipse.

All interest was now political, and the centre of the stage once more became those talk-ridden halls of the Duma where Moderate and Extremist were locked in what seemed to be a hopeless struggle. To the disinterested observer this controversy seemed almost ridiculous. In less than a week the most oppressed people in the world had shaken off the oppressor, and yet here they were fighting each other verbally with the same animosity and bitterness that they had hurled upon the tyrant a few days before.

All through that fateful Wednesday night, when the Czar was wrestling with his destiny down at Pskoff, the Duma remained in continuous and acrimonious session.

When Thursday broke it found the city quiet and many of the shops open. The trams, however, had not yet resumed operations. Men, women, and children wore red ribbons, and even the harness of the horses was decorated with crimson rosettes. When the street cars did begin to run again a few days later they flew red flags from the roofs.

The whole community was now divided into two hostile camps. One of them, dominated by the Duma, advocated a Constitutional Government under the Regency of the Grand Duke Michael; the other, inflamed by the Council of Workmen's and Soldiers' Delegates, cried for a Red Republic.

The Labourites still flooded the town with their seditious literature, while the Duma daily put forth its plea for constructive harmony. Freedom, gained at the cost of blood and agony, was being dashed back and forth like a tennis-ball on a hotly contested court. Even compromise seemed remote.

But those masterful men who had made the Revolution possible were guiding the new craft of State through the troubled waters. While leaders like Gutchkoff and Lvoff were manning the walls of the Duma, their colleagues were fashioning the new Ministry.

On Thursday afternoon came a great moment. It was when Milyukoff announced the members of the Provisional Government in a speech which took rank with that other historic utterance when he laid bare the infamy of the old Cabinet and proved the treason of the men responsible for national safety. But on this occasion he had a different tale to tell. It was no longer the sensational revelation of illicit relationship. He now had a message of cheer and confidence for his freed people.

The Cabinet which was revealed for the first time was composed of the following:

Prince George Lvoff, Premier and Minister of the Interior; Paul Milyukoff, Minister of Foreign Affairs; Alexander Gutchkoff, Minister of War and Marine; Alexander Kerensky, Minister of Justice; Michael Tereshtchenko, Minister of Finance; Andrew Shingarieff, Minister of Agriculture; Alexander Konovaloff, Minister of Commerce and Industries; Nicholas

Niekrasoff, Minister of Ways and Communication; Alexander Manuiloff, Minister of Public Instruction; Ivan Godneff, State Comptroller; Vladimir Lvoff, Over Procurator of the Holy Synod; Theodore Rodicheff, Minister of Finnish Affairs.

It was an impressive roster of achievement, for every member had been tested in the fires and had borne the ordeal of the battle for liberty. After he had revealed the names of his colleagues, Milyukoff continued:

"I hear voices ask: 'Who chose you?' No one chose us, for if we had waited for election by the people we could not wrench the power from the hands of the enemy. While we quarrel about who shall be elected the foe would have time to reorganise and reconquer both you and us. We were elected by the Russian Revolution. It so happened at the very moment when delay was impossible, a handful of people was found whose political past was well known to the people, and against whom not a shadow of those suspicions which brought the old Administration to its fall could be entertained, but we cannot forget that we ourselves quite recently defended the principle of responsibility of the Government to the electors.

"We shall not retain power for a single moment when we are told by the elected representatives of the people that they wish to see others, more deserving of their confidence, in our place. Believe me, Gentlemen, the Government will fight in these coming days not for the sake of power. To be in power is neither a reward nor a pleasure, but a merit and a sacrifice. And as soon as we are told that this sacrifice is no longer needed by the people we shall give up our place with gratitude for the opportunity which has been accorded us. But we will not relinquish power now when it is needed to consolidate the people's triumph, and when, should the power fall from our hands, it would only be seized by the foe."

Milyukoff also repeated a statement that he had made on other occasions during the past few days—namely, "that the despot who had brought Russia to the brink of ruin would either abdicate of his own free will or be deposed. The power will pass to

a Regent, the Grand Duke Michael Alexandrovitch, and Alexis will be the successor
to the Throne."

Now the extraordinary feature of this
speech was that, while Milyukoff was making it, the Czar had abdicated and was on
his way to Tsarskoe Selo. The news did
not reach Petrograd, however, until that
night, when cheering crowds read it in
flaming letters on the walls.

Milyukoff now became the storm centre.
His declaration about a Regent, which he
was forced to admit later was purely his
personal opinion, stirred up a hornet's nest.
In the swift change from servile depend-
ency to rampant liberty the pendulum had
swung completely round. A few weeks before, the thought of a Regent would have
been hailed by the multitude as a blessing
from Heaven; now it meant tyranny and
oppression.

The Council of Workmen's and Soldiers'
Delegates swept completely out of bounds.
It seemed to lose all restraint.

"We want a Republic and we must have
it at once," was the cry.

Again the magnetic Kerensky saved the

hour. Leaping upon a table in the middle of the hall he shouted:

"Comrades, I have been made Minister of Justice, but in entering the Provisional Government I remain a Republican. In my work I must lean for help upon the will of the people. May I trust you as I trust myself?"

At this there was tremendous cheering and cries of "We believe you, comrade."

Then he continued:

"I cannot live without the people, and if ever you begin to doubt me, kill me. I declare to the Provisional Government that I am a representative of the Democracy, and that the Government must especially take into account the views I shall uphold as representing the people, by whose efforts the old Government was overthrown. Comrades, time does not wait. I call you to organisation and discipline. I ask you to support us, your representatives, who are prepared to die for the people, and have given the people their whole life."

His fervour swept all before it. The Democrats voted to support the Provisional Government until the end of the war. One peril to the new order was gone.

But even the Conservatives realised that the atmosphere must be cleared of all royal taint, and thus came the final scene in the tragedy of the Romanoffs. A Committee, headed by Prince Lvoff, and including Kerensky, went to seek the Grand Duke Michael, and found him in the apartments of Prince Putiatin. He still believed himself the destined Regent of Russia.

"We are the bearers of the will of the people," said Kerensky.

"What is that will?" asked the Grand Duke, unconscious of the bolt about to be delivered.

"That you renounce the Regency and relegate all plenary powers to the Provisional Government until a Constituent Assembly, elected on a basis of universal and equal suffrage, decides upon the form of government," was the reply.

Michael looked dazed. It was the death blow to the old régime. Like Nicholas, at Pskoff, he nodded his head in humble and silent assent. The following declaration from the Throne was then dictated by Prince Lvoff:

"A heavy task has been entrusted to me by the will of my brother, who has given me the Imperial Throne at a time of unprecedented war and of domestic strife.

"Animated by the same feelings as the entire nation—namely, that the welfare of the country overshadows all other interests—I am firmly resolved to accept the Supreme Power only if this should be the desire of our great people, who must, by means of a plebiscite, through their representatives in the Constituent Assembly, establish the form of government and the new fundamental laws of the Russian State.

"Invoking God's blessing, I therefore request all citizens of Russia to obey the Provisional Government set up on the initiative of the Duma and invested with plenary powers, until, within as short a time as possible, the Constituent Assembly, elected on a basis of equal universal and secret suffrage, shall express the will of the nation regarding the form of government to be adopted."

Michael signed it, and when the ink of the signature was dry Russian royalty had passed into the shadow. In that moment the simple apartment, through whose windows came the sound of "The Marseillaise," sung by joyous crowds, took rank with Runnymede and Independence Hall.

Having temporarily bridged the chasm that threatened all manner of civil disruption, the Ministry proceeded to the colossal task of gathering up the frenzied and scattered threads of government.

Its first important manifesto was typical of the vision of the men who framed it. It was the herald of the New Russia, and it not only rang with conviction and purpose, but was a battle-cry to construction. Here it is in full:

"Citizens!

"The great work has been accomplished. By a powerful stroke the Russian people has overthrown the old régime. A new Russia is born. This *coup d'état* has set the keystone upon the long years of struggle. Under the pressure of the awakened forces the Act of October 30th, 1905, promised Russia constitutional liberties which, however, were not put into effect.

"The First Duma, the mouthpiece of the wishes of the nation, was dissolved. The Second Duma met with a similar fate, and the Government, being powerless to crush the national will, decided by the Act of June 16th, 1907, to withdraw from the people part of the legislative rights which had been promised them. During the ten succeeding years the Government withdrew from the people one after another all the rights they had won. The country was again thrown into the abyss of absolute rule and administrative arbitrariness.

"All attempts to make the voice of Reason heard were in vain, and the great world struggle into which our country was plunged found it face to face with the moral decadence of a power not united with the people, a power indifferent to the destinies of the country and steeped in vices and infamy. The heroic efforts of the Army crushed under the cruel weights of internal disorganisation, the appeals of the national representatives who united in view of the national danger, were powerless to lead the ex-Emperor and his Government into the path of union with the people.

"Thus when Russia, by the illegal and disastrous acts of her governors, was faced with the greatest disasters, the people had to take the power into their own hands. The unanimous revolutionary spirit of the people, fully realising the seriousness of the moment, and the firm will of the Duma, established a Provisional Government, which considers it its sacred duty to realise the national desires and to lead the country into the bright path of free civil organisation.

"The Government believes that the lofty spirit of patriotism, which the people have shown in the struggle against the old régime, will also animate our gallant soldiers in the fields of battle. On its side, the Government will do its utmost to provide the Army with all that is necessary to bring the war to a victorious conclusion.

"The Government will faithfully observe all the alliances uniting us to other Powers and all agreements made in the past. Whilst taking the measures indispensable for the defence of the country against the foreign enemy, the Government will consider it its first duty to grant the people every facility for expressing its will as to the political

régime, and will convoke as soon as possible
a Constituent Assembly on the basis of universal suffrage, at the same time assuring
the gallant defenders of the country their
share in the Parliamentary elections. The
Constituent Assembly will also issue fundamental laws guaranteeing the country the
immutable rights of equality and liberty.

"Conscious of all the burden of political
oppression weighing on the country and
hindering the free creative forces of the
people in a year of heavy trials, the Provisional Government deems it necessary, even
before the convocation of the Constituent
Assembly, to announce immediately to the
country its set principles assuring political
liberty and equality, in order to enable all
citizens to develop their strength in creative
work for the good of the country.

"The Government will be careful to lay
down principles assuring the participation
of all citizens in the communal elections,
which will be held on a basis of universal
suffrage.

"In the moment of national liberation
the whole country remembers with deep
gratitude the services of those who fell in

the struggle for their political and religious
ideas, to the vengeance of the old régime,
and the Provisional Government will joy-
fully facilitate the return from exile and
prison of all who are suffering for the good
of their country. In solving these problems
the Provisional Government believes that it
will be carrying out the national will, and
that the whole people will support it in its
efforts to secure the happiness of Russia."

Now that the reins of government had
been transferred to accredited hands, the
Duma adjourned after a career that will
take unique place in the history of all legislative procedure. Without this body, which
for years had been regarded as a Parliamentary joke, the Revolution would not only
have been improbable but impossible. The
Council of Workmen's and Soldiers' Delegates remained in session and their deliberations soon became fraught with dire consequence for Russia.

The new Ministry resumed work. So
complete had been the revolutionary overthrow that practically every public office of
any consequence was denuded. The students

of Democracy, therefore, were called upon
to give practical demonstration of their
theories. Most of them, however—men like
Tereshtchenko and Konovaloff—came to
their posts from experience in the conduct
of large business affairs. In the same way
Prince Lvoff, who had been head of the
Zemstvos and associated with the War Industry Committee, was a trained administra-
tor. There was a peculiar and poetic justice in
his assumption of the portfolio of the Interior because the man he succeeded, Protopopoff, had been his special oppressor, and had
blocked his public-spirited work at every turn.

The first idea of the new Government was
to get in close touch with the great mass of
the people and the Army in the field. Gutchkoff went off to visit the various Fronts and
made speeches up and down the line urging
the men to observe discipline and be loyal
to the New Russia. General Alexieff, the
brilliant Chief of Staff—a sergeant-son like
Sir William Robertson—became Command-
er-in-Chief of all the Forces in the field.
Here was another amazing example of the
concession at once made by the Government
to the popular clamour against royalty. In

the early days of the Revolution the Grand
Duke Nicholas, who had the confidence of
all the troops, was designated Commander-
in-Chief of the Imperial Forces. It was an
admirable choice, but his blue blood operated
against him, and he was succeeded by the
commoner who had risen from the ranks.

That the new régime meant business was
evident by the swift and efficient reorganisation of many of the departments, notably
that of Commerce and Industry. Within a
week after the Cabinet had been named
Konovaloff had effected an organisation,
and within four weeks after the last shot of
revolt was fired he had made a contract
with a large American Corporation for an
immense quantity of electric equipment for
the Government.

No revelation of the aftermath of the
Revolution was more characteristic of the
mood of the people than the utter and complete contempt shown for the Czar. The
humblest labourer, who a short time before
mentioned the royal name in hushed and
reverent whisper, now referred to him as
"Nicholas," and spat as he spoke.

Freedom indeed had come to Russia.

PETROGRAD was the real battle-
ground of the Revolution, and with
the cessation of actual hostilities it
became a throbbing theatre of emotion. Not since Paris raved in the first de-
lirium of Democracy has any world capital
witnessed such scenes. All rank was levelled
before the flood-tide of rejoicing that swept
the city.

I was with the Russian people while they
were making appraisal of their new assets.
Like prisoners long immured in the dark and
suddenly hurled into the sunshine, the people blinked in the strange light of their unfamiliar emancipation. The one-time baili-
wick of the Czar was a study in scarlet-ani-
mate like an American city during National
Convention. The Nevsky Prospect, once the
Street of Sacrifice, was now the Highway
of Happiness.

Never was there such glad reunion; it
was like a meeting of lost tribes after
much wandering in the wilderness. Exiles

streamed in from Siberia under the general amnesty; Jews came forth from their long restraint for creed lines were down; delegations of troops flocked from the Front. Equality was the password that loosed every tongue.

Over the Winter Palace, around which the waves of piteous anguish had so often surged in vain appeal, waved the flag of Revolution. Even the imperial eagles on the huge iron gates—closed forever on royalty—were swathed in red rags!

Everybody talked, paraded, had a theory or a programme. The voice of Russia, long stifled, was making up for lost time. Freedom was a new sensation, and the populace revelled in it proud, sensitive, elated—afraid that it might disappear like a dream. The town buzzed like a Babel. It was a whirlwind of plan and project.

"Can order and economic permanency come out of this chaos?" I asked Kerensky.

"Certainly," he replied. "I will tell you why. Is not this healthy if heated discussion which dissolves in the air in harmless oratory better than sinister and silent plots? Our people have just discovered that they have a voice. They are learning to use it—straining it perhaps in the fear that it might be suppressed before they can say all they want to say. When they learn that they are free to talk they will subside and get down to normal life again."

I looked in vain for a policeman. There was no such animal. So far as Petrograd—indeed all Russia—was concerned, the species was extinct. Instead you saw an occasional student or civilian with a white brassard on his sleeve and carrying a gun—a militiaman—who represented law. But he was not needed.

Here you got evidence of a real popular rule. Authority by, and for, the people was here. The citizens had become mentors of their own conduct—on honour as it were—and faithful to the trust they imposed upon themselves.

What was happening in Petrograd during those blithe days of April awakening was being duplicated throughout the length and breadth of that far-flung land. Everywhere the police had been banished to the Front to do a man's work. Russia breathed freely.

In the capital you saw signs of the price

paid for this freedom. Remnants of barricades still littered the streets, mottling the snow were dark spots that spelled disaster, bullet-holes gaped from walls like ugly sockets.

But death and destruction were part of the hideous Yesterday. The thought was of the glad To-day with its daybreak of hope and its rich promise of a constructive To-morrow.

A new Petrograd stood revealed. The man who had seen it under the iron heel of Autocracy rubbed his eyes. Privates passed Generals without saluting; every conceivable kind of incendiary pamphlet was sold on the sidewalk and without restraint; vendors hawked booklets that flashed the picture of Rasputin caricatured.

You walked past the Winter Palace and you saw knots of curious people staring in at the gardens or assembled under the *portecochère*. A month before it would have been worth a civilan's life to loiter, even for a moment, within a hundred yards of the sacred entrance.

Order which had vied with liberty as the watchword of Revolution remained, as one

amazing incident showed. It was the great
public funeral of the civilian victims of the
police. Many people who had marvelled at
the miracle of the insurrection ceased to
wonder when they saw those lurid obsequies.

According to the most conservative esti-
mates, about five hundred civilians were
killed during the fighting in Petrograd. The
total number of casualties was less than five
thousand. A number of the victims were
privately buried by their families, but nearly
two hundred bodies of revolutionists were
kept for the spectacular tribute which was
to give the Russian the opportunity of rendering homage to his martyred dead and
likewise indulging in the characteristic love
of ceremony.

It was held on a bleak April day, under
lowering grey skies, and in a city ankle deep
in slush. For a week the coming event was
on every tongue.

"But," said the alarmists, the day before
the funeral, "the city will pay dearly for
the show. These martyrs will have new
companions for their delayed last journey."

Dire predictions of the wreaking of the
deferred vengeance certain to be inflamed

and excited by the sight of the dead, to say nothing of the possibility of a panic-producing attack on the crowd by some secret police who may have survived the storm, rose up: "Keep off the streets," was the warning to the stranger. No one heeded it.

As in the Revolution itself the unexpected happened. With perfect discipline the million marched and wept. A community, once police-ridden, and still quivering with rage at incessant wrongs, kept the peace almost without sign of authority. It augured well for the stability of the new régime.

On that day fury yielded to tenderness, and you saw enacted the sentimental climax of the epic of freedom that had startled the world. It was a funeral such as no time had ever seen before or is likely to witness again. There was no panoply of pomp or purple, no sombre trapping of woe. The brilliant red of protest and passion, emblem of the new-found freedom, flashed on a thousand banners, shone from the caskets that held the martyred dead, ran like a flame up and down the unending lines of civilians and soldiers that tramped from dawn to dark. A hundred bands sobbed with Cho-

STUDENTS AND CIVILIANS CARRYING THE BODIES
OF COMRADES TO THE COMMON GRAVE

ALL THE VICTIMS OF THE REVOLUTION WERE
BURIED IN RED CASKETS IN ONE HUGE GRAVE

pin's Funeral March; a hundred thousand voices gave "The Marseillaise" a thrilling intensity that smote the heart.

On the Field of Mars a common grave became the sanctuary and the symbol of sacrifice. Around it the nation mourned yet rejoiced.

This unforgettable spectacle, with its crimson coffins, its singing multitudes, and its haunting solemnity was more than a picturesque burial. It was one definite reason why the Great Upheaval of a few weeks before had achieved the downfall of Czardom.

The crusading spirit that thrilled it, the amazing order that pervaded it, the high sense of dignity and reverence that well-nigh exalted it, disclosed those larger forces, long unreckoned with, that had expanded a hunger riot almost overnight into an uprising and uprooted a dynasty.

Not a voice was raised save in prayer or chant; no hand stretched forth but to serve. The threatened Commune became a Public Confessional of serene sorrow. Grief, that unfailing crystalliser of character, had done more in a single day to illume the most memorable chapter of Russian history than a century of chroniclers. The restraint that had tempered wrath in the high tides of revolt stood revealed, and with it the supreme gifts of patience and forbearance.

Petrograd was as safe as a Sunday School Convention. As if emblazoned on those waving banners, shone the explanation why the Revolution had been comparatively bloodless—why it had been complete—why the whole structure of the dawning Russian Republic, heedless of the social and economic storms that will inevitably break about it, was secure.

There were other evidences of the order which seemed to be the hall-mark of the Revolution. Every bank was guarded by soldiers day and night, and there was an armed guard in all the hotels. There was little or no looting. Stringent orders had been issued for the summary re-arrest of the criminals who had escaped with the general dropping of prison bars, and most of them were returned to custody. Some persons who were in stolen uniforms entered and ransacked a few private houses, but they were promptly caught and shot. As a protection

against these raids, a Committee of Safety
was formed in every apartment house, and
the men, armed with guns provided by the
Provisional Government, took turns on
watch all night long. Each man was on duty
for two hours.

A very commendable sort of every-day
justice prevailed. For one thing, the motor
cars seized during the Revolution were returned to their owners. In cases where
damage had been done to the cars there was
prompt indemnity.

No phase of those stirring days of transition was more impressive than the tone of
the uncensored press. The newspapers re-
appeared after a week's silence, and the
news-dealers were almost overwhelmed by
the news-hungry populace. The whole tone
of the journals was uniformly patriotic in
the highest degree. There was a unanimous
emphasis in pointing out the fact that while
freedom had been obtained with slight sacrifice of life, enormous difficulties lay in the
path of the new Government. For several
weeks, even the most radical sheets advocated counsels of prudence and moderation.
Indeed, never was censorship so admirably

applied as the self-imposed censorship of the Petrograd newspapers in those first weeks that followed the Revolution.

In that quick procession of unfolding wonders you were surprised at nothing. For the first time in the long and dismal story of racial oppression, the Jew held up his head proudly, and walked the streets erect and unafraid. Under the new mantle of freedom, Hebrew and Gentile were linked in the common brotherhood of privilege.

While the people were still binding up the wounds of battle, their eyes and their souls turned to the finer things. Under the Chairmanship of Maxim Gorky, a Committee on Arts and Letters was formed for the special purpose of safeguarding the works of art. Already the poet and the dreamer had a vision of a new art and a new literature, shot through with the great fire of freedom.

One fly in the ointment of all this equality was the let-down in discipline among the soldiers. Fresh from the British front in France, the conspicuous indifference that the private soldier showed to the commonest courtesy of the army struck me as little short of shocking. I saw venerable generals,

with the wound and service stripes of two
wars on their sleeves, hanging by the strap
of the tramcars while every seat was occupied by a grinning and sometimes jeering
common soldier. The soldiers' adhesion had
turned the scale of the Revolution; he knew
it and he was capitalising his importance.

You did not have to travel far to know
that the Russian soldier in Petrograd was
having the time of his life. With that amiable and childlike simplicity for which he is
noted, he played the new game of freedom
for all it was worth. Under the new order,
soldiers could ride free of charge on the
tramcars and on the railways. Life now became one constant trip for the Tommy.
Troopers who had never been on trains in
their lives until they were called to the
colours now began to visit all their friends
and relatives.

For the ordinary civilian travel became a
great adventure, and likewise a constant
hardship and inconvenience.

A member of the British Embassy staff at
Petrograd engaged and paid for a coupé to
Moscow. He was going on official business,
and it was most important for him to leave

on a certain night. When he reached the train he found the compartment occupied by eight Russian soldiers.

"I am very sorry to disturb you," said the Englishman, who spoke Russian fluently, "but this is my coupé; I am going to Moscow on official business." He showed his ticket, whereupon one of the Russians immediately replied:

"It is all right. We have not the slightest objection to your riding down with us."

There was no ill-will or hostility in any of these performances. It was all part of a good-natured debauch of democracy.

The situation in Petrograd was not without its humour. The disdain for the Czar became more pronounced every day. One morning I read in the newspapers that citizen Ivan Romanoff had solemnly petitioned the Duma for permission to change his name to Ivan Republicanitskey. He was determined that his posterity should not bear the hated label of royalty.

Before the Revolution, Petrograd had been a portrait gallery of the Royal Family. Now it was alive with the photographs of the Revolution-makers. Every picture of the Czar had been banned to the garbage heap; to try to buy one was arch-treason. Where portraits of the Emperor could not be removed—such as those in the Chamber of the Council of Empire—they were covered with white crêpe.

The eagle—emblem of imperial power, but likewise the symbol of American freedom—had a hard time. His day of trouble began, for he was wrenched from every flagpole and removed from every arch. An American manufacturing firm, whose imposing building on the Nevsky was surmounted by a huge iron eagle, was compelled to drape the proud bird in the Stars and Stripes until only the beak protruded from the red, white, and blue folds.

Amid this carnival of equality were signs of some realisation of economic responsibility. Nothing was more characteristic than the Loan of Liberty. Scarcely had the shock of revolution passed than the cry rose up among sober-minded men: "Let us try to pay our way as much as possible." A great popular subscription was launched for a five per cent. bond issued at 85, and redeemable in forty years.

Petrograd was placarded from end to end with announcements of the loan, which were also fastened to turrets and even to the guns of armoured cars which were sent racing through the streets, a reminder of the days of bloody battle when they were in the thick of the fighting.

The newspapers carried full-page manifestoes from the Provisional Government urging the people to subscribe. They embodied such a fine and patriotic appeal that the first one is well worth reproducing. It read:

"To you citizens of Great Emancipated Russia and to those of you to whom the future of our country is dear, we make a passionate appeal.

"The powerful foe has forced his way deep into our territories; he threatens to crush us and to return us to the old régime which is now dead.

"Only the accumulation of all our strength can give us the victory which we desire. To save the country and complete the structure of an Emancipated Russia on a basis of equality and right the expenditure of many milliards is necessary. Our country demands this, not as a sacrifice but as the fulfilment of a duty. In subscribing to the new loan we will lend money to the State, and by this act we will save our freedom and our property from perishing."

But all was not merry-making in Petrograd's rejoicing. Up through the froth of those hectic days poked the head of Labour, shaking its locks at Capital, and inaugurating a reign of discontent that soon came perilously near national disaster.

Equality, like strong drink, went to the worker's head. He seemed to lose his whole sense of proportion. After the fateful week of fighting, and still another week of parading, he went back to his shop—but not to work. He became an agitator, with a string of demands that staggered the employer.

He saw the soldiers dismissing their officers and appointing their own superiors by popular vote, so he said, "We must do likewise, we will have no more foremen. Industry must be democratised like the army."

There was only one result—diminished output and near demoralisation. Sixty per cent. of the munition plants of Russia are in the Petrograd district, and the effect on war operations may be well imagined.

The situation went to an extreme that rivalled the old reign of reaction. The employers naturally expected requests for wage increases, but the demands now made were almost beyond belief. No advance was less than fifty per cent., while the average was from one hundred to one hundred and fifty. In one shipyard, for example, the workers insisted upon an increase of forty-five per cent. in all back pay from the beginning of the War, and an advance of one hundred per cent. from the first day of the Revolution. In still another industrial establishment the increase in wages asked would have swollen the annual expenditure by 13,000,-000 roubles. Most of the excessive demands were refused, and the workers struck. During the first four weeks following the Revolution half the mills in and about Petrograd were idle.

It was a different strike, however, from the historic walk-out of 1905, which was the prelude to a costly and ineffectual protest against the iron despotism. Now the victory had been won and Labour was in the throes of jubilant if exorbitant celebration.

With the demand for increased wages came its full brother—a demand for decrease in the working time. In some factories the workmen went to the well-nigh incredible extent of asking for a six-hour day with a nine-hour wage. Some workers blankly refused to work more than four hours per day. The most sober-minded element of Labour, however, united for a standard eight-hour day.

The whole industrial world seemed uprooted. The situation became so acute that the representatives of eighty-nine companies of the Petrograd garrison presented a formal request to the workmen to cease party strife and quarrels with technical experts and factory administrations, and to present their economic demands only through the medium of the arbitration courts and the Council of Workmen's and Soldiers' Delegates, and even postpone the introduction of an eight-hour day in the interests of the Russian army.

Thus a new and dangerous element was

introduced, namely, the interference of the
army in public political and economic life.
So far this interference was only verbal,
however.

Out of this interference came a very
dramatic episode. A group of soldiers went
to a meeting of striking workmen who were
vociferously clamouring for an eight-hour
day and an increase of one hundred per cent.
in wages.

"Why are you demanding the eight-hour
day?" asked the spokesman of the soldiers,
every one of whom wore the Cross of St.
George, which is the Russian Victoria Cross.

"Because eight hours is long enough for
any one to work," was the reply.

"We work all the time and our lives are
in constant danger," responded the soldier.

"But we must have more money," cried
one of the Socialist workmen.

The spokesman for the soldiers tore the
medals from his breast and flung them down
on the table, followed in turn by every one
of his colleagues.

"These medals," said the fighting man,
"represent sacrifice and blood. Sell them
and get money. But we must have shells."

This rebuke shamed the men to such a degree that hundreds went back to work at once. But they were in the minority.

The extremes to which Labour went were ludicrous. Even the housemaids struck. They organised a huge demonstration, left their saucepans and brooms and paraded the streets for days, waving red flags and shouting for increased wages and for shorter hours. This picturesque protest developed many humorous incidents. A housemaid in the employ of a well-known American resident in Petrograd served notice on her master that she wanted an increase of fifty per cent. in wages and an eight-hour day.

"What do you mean by an eight-hour day?" asked her employer.

"I am only going to work from eight until eight," was the reply. Her demand was speedily granted.

The postmen said: "Five deliveries a day are too many for Petrograd. Two are ample." They permitted 25,000,000 undelivered letters to pile up at the post offices, while 175 wagons filled with parcels post packages stood unopened at the railway terminals.

Labour's zeal was its undoing, as the following story will show: In a certain large factory the men sent a deputation to the employer—an American—with this ultimatum:

"We are all now free and equal, and we demand not only wages, but a share of your profits. We are as much the owner of your establishment as you are."

The American was swift of thought and swifter of action, so he replied:

"All right, I am glad to share the responsibility of my factory with you." Then, turning to his desk he produced a pile of papers, and handing them over to the spokesman said:

"Here are bills for thirty thousand roubles, due next Saturday. Will you be good enough to provide the money for them?"

The Delegation looked dazed. When it had caught its breath, the leader spoke up:

"We have no money for bills, that is your job."

"But how about your equal ownership? It also means equal responsibility of all kinds," queried the employer. The argument was unanswerable, and the men went back to work with no further outcry against private ownership.

THE MEMBERS OF THE CABINET AT THE BURIAL OF
THE VICTIMS OF THE REVOLUTION

THE RED CASKETS IN THE GRAVE

The disorganisation is best expressed by the following extract from a leading article in the *Russkaya Volya,* which contained the following:

"The present idleness is not the result of the Labour disturbances which were caused by the Revolution, and which naturally took the form of pressure on employers, with the object of improving the conditions of the workmen. This pressure is rapidly developing into an anti-social, anti-state, anti-patriotic, and anti-labour character.

"It would be foolish to imagine that the business can be confined to words if great reforms are not shortly made in the matter of organisation. Too much strain has been accumulated in the atmosphere, and too much energy held in check. It is of the first importance to draw the attention of the leaders of the Labour movement to this danger. If ruin comes, as it threatens to do, they will not be able to stand before it. It is essential that the Council of Workmen's and Soldiers' Delegates should use their weighty authority in the matter of restoring order. The Council must at least exert as much energy in this matter as they did in drawing up their resolution on the war.

"Otherwise, we are threatened with ruin, which will be made use of by the enemies of the new Constitution, and also by the German spies, so busy now stirring up strife. The present demagogy is twice as dangerous as the former, for with the right of free propaganda, and with public responsibility less restrained, any madman can profit by liberty to carry out his own wild plans."

Such was the picture of Petrograd in transition—a city ecstatic with equality. The soldiers were like children on a joyous holiday; the workers claimed all industry for their own. Before the people realised what was happening they were face to face with a grave crisis.

THE labour unrest that demoralised Petrograd was merely one phase of a larger disquiet which now shook the structure of the new Government to its foundations. Before the Provisional Ministry had firmly grasped the full meaning of its authority the Council of Workmen's and Soldiers' Delegates let loose a flood of destructive and disruptive demands. Its assembly hall became the forum of Radicalism that began to place every possible difficulty in the path of reconstruction.

Self-interest, which had been the doom of the deposed régime, took up its abode with the Dissenters. Forgetful of the fact that the Great War had made their freedom possible, they took steps to defeat the purpose of their Allies to bring that war to a successful end. Peace became the burden of their talk.

With this talk of peace was linked the plea for a very dangerous altruism which found expression in the slogan "Peace without Annexation." The anarchists found it a fruitful subject. They were led by Lenin, who had been an exile in Switzerland and had now returned to his native land. The very fact that Germany had permitted him to travel through her Empire was sufficient argument that his coming back to Petrograd was unfortunate to say the least. At first his treasonable plea for a peace at any price was received with some favour by the extremists, but to the everlasting credit of the best element of the Council he was finally ejected from their meetings. He tried to organise an anti-American demonstration—for the United States had just entered the war—and was finally suppressed. But not until he had planted pernicious seed.

Throughout Petrograd and more especially in the rabid wing of the Council of Workmen's and Soldiers' Delegates, men began to ask: "What has Russia to do with conquest? Democracy must be generous, even extravagant with the peace terms." These uplifters were quite oblivious to the fact that France—one of the most precious of all democracies—was even then under the despoiler's heel: that the hearts and the homes of millions of her people had been ravaged and that vast areas of her beloved land were in the grip of a merciless invader.

Some of the Socialists in the Council openly advocated fraternisation between Russian and German troops at the front. They even sent emissaries to the troops urging such an illicit intercourse. In some instances Russian soldiers went with white flags to their enemies for the purpose of discussing the truce. It was not only fatal to discipline, but it curbed the whole fighting spirit.

The Council clamoured for the publication of the secret treaties of the Russian Government with their Allies, unmindful of the immense benefit to the enemy that the dissemination of such information might bestow. It was during these turbulent days that Milyukoff incurred the hostility that led to his subsequent retirement from the capital. He not only resisted all efforts to disclose the terms of the treaties but insisted upon a reaffirmation of the principle that Russia must acquire Constantinople and the Dardanelles. At every turn he sought to thwart the desires of the Socialists whose sole idea was a peace without victory.

All this discussion, which was fully aired in the public press, had a most disturbing effect. For one thing it naturally created distrust and even suspicion among the Allies who at that moment were spilling their best blood on half a dozen fronts. It affected the morale of the Russian army to such an extent that Petrograd became almost panic-stricken at the fear of a German advance that would convert the capital into another Moscow, but without the penalty that Napoleon paid for that historic conflagration.

The situation became so alarming that the Government felt called upon to issue its famous Statement of April 9 on the Object of the War. Like many of the documents produced by that first group of patriots it was both noble and eloquent. It so clearly sets forth the ideas of the Cabinet and is at the same time such a notable state paper that I am reproducing it herewith in full:

"Citizens:

"The Provisional Government, surveying the military situation of Russia, in the name of its duty before country has decided frankly and openly to tell the nation the truth.

The disorganisation is best expressed by the following extract from a leading article in the *Russkaya Volya,* which contained the following:

"The present idleness is not the result of the Labour disturbances which were caused by the Revolution, and which naturally took the form of pressure on employers, with the object of improving the conditions of the workmen. This pressure is rapidly developing into an anti-social, anti-state, anti-patriotic, and anti-labour character.

"It would be foolish to imagine that the business can be confined to words if great reforms are not shortly made in the matter of organisation. Too much strain has been accumulated in the atmosphere, and too much energy held in check. It is of the first importance to draw the attention of the leaders of the Labour movement to this danger. If ruin comes, as it threatens to do, they will not be able to stand before it. It is essential that the Council of Workmen's and Soldiers' Delegates should use their weighty authority in the matter of restoring order. The Council must at least exert as much energy in this matter as they did in drawing up their resolution on the war.

"Otherwise, we are threatened with ruin, which will be made use of by the enemies of the new Constitution, and also by the German spies, so busy now stirring up strife. The present demagogy is twice as dangerous as the former, for with the right of free propaganda, and with public responsibility less restrained, any madman can profit by liberty to carry out his own wild plans."

Such was the picture of Petrograd in transition—a city ecstatic with equality. The soldiers were like children on a joyous holiday; the workers claimed all industry for their own. Before the people realised what was happening they were face to face with a grave crisis.

THE labour unrest that demoralised Petrograd was merely one phase of a larger disquiet which now shook the structure of the new Government to its foundations. Before the Provisional Ministry had firmly grasped the full meaning of its authority the Council of Workmen's and Soldiers' Delegates let loose a flood of destructive and disruptive demands. Its assembly hall became the forum of Radicalism that began to place every possible difficulty in the path of reconstruction.

Self-interest, which had been the doom of the deposed régime, took up its abode with the Dissenters. Forgetful of the fact that the Great War had made their freedom possible, they took steps to defeat the purpose of their Allies to bring that war to a successful end. Peace became the burden of their talk.

With this talk of peace was linked the plea for a very dangerous altruism which found expression in the slogan "Peace without Annexation." The anarchists found it a

fruitful subject. They were led by Lenin,
who had been an exile in Switzerland and
had now returned to his native land. The
very fact that Germany had permitted him
to travel through her Empire was sufficient
argument that his coming back to Petrograd
was unfortunate to say the least. At first
his treasonable plea for a peace at any price
was received with some favour by the extremists, but to the everlasting credit of the
best element of the Council he was finally
ejected from their meetings. He tried to
organise an anti-American demonstration—
for the United States had just entered the
war—and was finally suppressed. But not
until he had planted pernicious seed.

Throughout Petrograd and more especially in the rabid wing of the Council of
Workmen's and Soldiers' Delegates, men
began to ask: "What has Russia to do with
conquest? Democracy must be generous,
even extravagant with the peace terms."
These uplifters were quite oblivious to the
fact that France—one of the most precious
of all democracies—was even then under the
despoiler's heel: that the hearts and the
homes of millions of her people had been

ravaged and that vast areas of her beloved land were in the grip of a merciless invader.

Some of the Socialists in the Council openly advocated fraternisation between Russian and German troops at the front. They even sent emissaries to the troops urging such an illicit intercourse. In some instances Russian soldiers went with white flags to their enemies for the purpose of discussing the truce. It was not only fatal to discipline, but it curbed the whole fighting spirit.

The Council clamoured for the publication of the secret treaties of the Russian Government with their Allies, unmindful of the immense benefit to the enemy that the dissemination of such information might bestow. It was during these turbulent days that Milyukoff incurred the hostility that led to his subsequent retirement from the capital. He not only resisted all efforts to disclose the terms of the treaties but insisted upon a reaffirmation of the principle that Russia must acquire Constantinople and the Dardanelles. At every turn he sought to thwart the desires of the Socialists whose sole idea was a peace without victory.

All this discussion, which was fully aired in the public press, had a most disturbing effect. For one thing it naturally created distrust and even suspicion among the Allies who at that moment were spilling their best blood on half a dozen fronts. It affected the morale of the Russian army to such an extent that Petrograd became almost panic-stricken at the fear of a German advance that would convert the capital into another Moscow, but without the penalty that Napoleon paid for that historic conflagration.

The situation became so alarming that the Government felt called upon to issue its famous Statement of April 9 on the Object of the War. Like many of the documents produced by that first group of patriots it was both noble and eloquent. It so clearly sets forth the ideas of the Cabinet and is at the same time such a notable state paper that I am reproducing it herewith in full:

"Citizens:

"The Provisional Government, surveying the military situation of Russia, in the name of its duty before country has decided frankly and openly to tell the nation the truth.

"The late Government left the work of national defence utterly disorganized. By its criminal inactivity and inept measures it has brought us to the brink of destruction in our finances, on the questions of food and transport, and in the provisioning of the army. It has ruined the country economically.

"The Provisional Government, with the lively and active co-operation of the whole nation, is devoting all its energies to the task of reducing to order the baleful heritage left to it by the old régime. But time will not wait. The blood of many sons of the Fatherland has been poured out without measure during the two and a half years of war, but the country yet remains under the pressure of a powerful enemy, who has possessed itself of whole provinces of our state and now threatens us with a new and decisive onslaught.

"The defence at all cost of our national inheritance and the freeing of our country from the enemy who has invaded our frontiers—this is the first insistent and real task of our soldiers, the defending of the nation's freedom.

"Leaving the final decision of all questions connected with the world-war and its conclusions to the will of the people, in close union with our Allies, the Provisional Government considers it to be its right and duty now to declare the aims of emancipated Russia are not domination over other nations, not the filching from them of their property, not the acquisition of foreign territory by force of arms, but the consolidation of a lasting peace based on the establishment of nations within their natural limits. The Russian people are not striving to increase their outward power at the expense of other nations, slavery and humiliation find no place in that aim to which they devote their efforts. In the name of the highest principles of justice they have stricken their shackles from off the Polish people. But the Russian nation will not allow their country to issue from the struggle humiliated and with shattered strength. These principles are laid down as the foreign policy of the Provisional Government, conscientiously fulfilling the national will, guarding the rights of our country and fully observing the obligations owed to our Allies.

"The Provisional Government of free Russia has no right to hide the truth from the people. The state is in danger. We must do all in our power to save it. Let the answer of the country to the truth be no fruitless depression, no decline in our courage, but a universal impulse to the creation of a single national will. It will give us new strength for the struggle and will lead us to salvation.

"In the hour of heavy trial let the whole country find itself strength to maintain our conquered freedom and devote itself to unceasing labour for the good of emancipated Russia. The Provisional Government who have taken a solemn oath to serve the people, firmly believe that it, with the general and unanimous support of all and every one, will itself also be able to fulfil its duty to the country until the end."

To the great mass of people in Petrograd and elsewhere in Russia this manifest brought a sobering realisation of the gravity of conditions. "The state is in danger" was no idle phrase devised to put the fear of God into the hearts of the insurgents. It was the plain brutal truth and it meant that the enemy at the frontier was no worse than the enemy at home.

Instead of placating the red element of the Council of Workmen's and Soldiers' Delegates this appeal only inflamed them. They sought fresh powers. Amazing as it may seem they now demanded that all military operations be submitted to their Executive Committee. It meant, if carried out, that every bit of strategy proposed by the generals in the field would have to be debated over by a group of men whose only contact with war had been abuse of the methods employed by the Government. It was monstrous and it was unreasonable.

When the Duma met in extraordinary session to celebrate the anniversary of the

opening of the first Russian Parliament,
Gutchkoff, the Minister of War, gave utterance to the indignation of the great mass of
the people when he made this startling statement:

"We must frankly face the fact that our military might is weakened and disintegrated, being
affected by the same disease as the country—
namely, duality of power, polyarchy, anarchy—
only the malady is more acute. This disease
constitutes a mortal danger for the State and for
the nation. It is not too late to cure it, but not
a moment must be lost.

"Those who, either deliberately or not realising what they were doing, have cast into our
midst the subversive catchword, 'Peace at the
front and war in the country'—these people, I
say, are carrying on a propaganda of peace at
any price and civil war, cost what it may. That
word must be smothered by another, 'War at
the front and peace within the country.'

"Some time ago the country realised that our
motherland was in danger. Since then we have
gone a step further, for our motherland is on the
edge of an abyss."

Still the Dissenters persisted in their
policy of antagonism and interference.
They tried in every possible way to distract

the Government and more particularly the Ministry of War and Marine from instituting an adequate state of National Defence. The inevitable happened for Gutchkoff resigned his post. In making announcement of his retirement he gave the following illuminating reason:

"In view of the conditions in which the power of the Government is placed, especially the authority of the Ministry of War in relation to the Army and Navy, conditions which I am powerless to alter, and which threaten to have consequences fatal to the defence of the liberty and even the existence of Russia, I can no longer exercise the functions of Minister of War and Marine and share the responsibility for the grave sin that is being committed against the country."

It was the first break in the Cabinet that was to be the bulwark of the New Liberty. The crack had come. Would the whole fabric of the Provisional Government totter? Sober-minded people trembled for the future of the infant democracy.

Hardly had the sensation produced by Gutchkoff's resignation subsided than the news broke that General Brusiloff, who had commanded the Russian armies in the great

Galician offensive and who was a real national hero, had asked to be relieved of his command. This defection was swiftly followed by the resignations of General Russky and General Gurko.

"What will come next?" asked the now thoroughly alarmed people. They were not long in finding out.

A group of Socialists went to Schluesselburg near Petrograd, seat of one of the largest of the Russian powder factories and employing more than 10,000 men, and tried to set up an autonomous republic defying the Provisional Government.

A counter revolution seemed imminent. The spectre of a New Russia composed of numerous small and conflicting republics rose over the horizon.

Nor were German agents slow to reap a harvest out of this whirlpool of disorder. Many Prussian agents had escaped the comb of the Revolution and others were able to get to the country in the early days of the upheaval when the frontiers were as open gates. They plied an industrious and devastating propaganda. Petrograd was like an asp that sucked the life's blood of freedom.

It was this condition that led Kerensky to ask: "Is it a case that Free Russia has become a state of revolted slaves? We have taken a sip of freedom and it has intoxicated us."

The anomalous situation could not continue. Anarchy loomed dark amid the encircling chaos. It was too late for a greathearted Lincoln to bind the conflicting factions. The conviction began to grow that Russia could only be saved by the ruthlessness and the resolution of a Cromwell. It was a choice between dictatorship and disintegration.

At the moment when despair was darkest and when only a hair's breadth seemed to separate the Provisional Government from a new Socialistic régime, the whole problem was solved with dramatic swiftness. Once more it was Kerensky who saved the hour. He made an impassioned plea for conciliation to the Executive Committee of the Council of Workmen's and Soldiers' Delegates and by a vote of forty-one to nineteen it decided in favour of a participation by the

Socialistic parties with the Provisional Government. Whatever might now happen there was at least unity of action among the forces that controlled the country.

After an all-night session between the Executive Committee of the Council of Workmen's and Soldiers' Delegates, the Ministry and the Executive Committee of the Duma, the fundamental principles forming the basis of the new co-operation were decided on. They were:

"Active foreign policy directed towards the speediest possible attainment of general peace without annexation or indemnity based on the express will of the people, and negotiations with the Allies for a revision of their agreements with Russia on the basis of the declaration of the Provisional Government of April 9th.

"Democratisation of the Army and improvement in fighting effectiveness at the front for proper defence of Russian freedom.

"Re-establishment of internal order by State control of food supplies and transport.

"Agrarian policy on basis of land for the people.

"Reorganisation of existing financial system with a view to the transference of the burden of taxation to the wealthy and property-owning classes.

"Earliest possible meeting of the Constituent Assembly.

"Socialist Ministers to be responsible to the Council of Workmen's and Soldiers' Delegates, and not to the Provisional Government."

This programme of policy necessitated great concessions to the Socialists, but they were an indispensable condition of social-istic collaboration with the Government. It was a desperate case that required an equally desperate remedy. Russia had to be saved from the anarchy which had already cast its shadow over the land.

A Coalition Cabinet—the agency that saved Great Britain during the dark days of 1916—now came to the rescue of racked Russia. The national carpenters began their work and there was a mighty hammer-ing. The Socialists had been promised six portfolios in the re-organised government and this meant that somebody had to be displaced.

But before the shake-up began the veteran Milyukoff resigned as Minister of Foreign Affairs. His retirement was one of the conditions of Socialistic co-operation. His views on the subject of Russia's interna-

tional obligations were too strong for the
Radical stomach. With that fine sense of
unswerving loyalty which had marked the
long years of his devotion to the cause of
freedom, he pledged his services to the new
order and urged his Constitutional Democratic colleagues in the Cabinet—Shingareff
and Manuiloff—to remain at their posts.
He was succeeded by Tereshtchenko, whose
office as Minister of Finance was assumed
by Shingareff.

The miracle of the re-organised Government was the shifting of Kerensky from the
Ministry of Justice to the War Portfolio.
A Socialist and a Labourite was in the seat
of Mars! It was typical of the destiny of
this remarkable man that in assuming this
most difficult of all the cabinet posts he really
assumed responsibility for the future of
Russia. The re-constituted cabinet included
nine of the old Ministers. Five new posts
were created—Labour, Public Relief, Food
Supplies, Posts and Telegraphs, and a Department for the Affairs of the Constituent
Assembly which is to be convened in Petrograd at the earliest possible moment. As

re-organised the Cabinet presented the following personnel:

Prince George Lvoff, Prime Minister and Interior; Tereshtchenko, Foreign Affairs; Kerensky, War and Marine; Shingareff, Finance; Nekrasoff, Railways; Konavoloff, Commerce; Godneff, State Controller; Manuiloff, Education; Vladimir Lvoff, Holy Synod; Pereveizeff, Justice; Skobeleff, Labour; Tchernoff, Agriculture; Tseretelli, Posts and Telegraphs; Pietchekhonoff, Food Supplies; Shakhovskoy, Public Relief; Grimm, Constituent Affairs.

Although they came from the domain of discord the new Ministers were proved and seasoned organisers for they really represented the best element in the Council of Workmen's and Soldiers' Delegates. Skobeleff, for example, had been Vice-President and had great capacity for quick decision. While Tchernoff has been for fifteen years on the Executive Committee of the Social Democratic party, which defied government espionage and effected a far-reaching organisation extending to the smallest villages. He is a leader in the Russian co-operative movement and his presence in the Cabinet when the inevitable question of land settlement arises means that the peasant will have a strong friend at court. In the same way Tseretelli had been a conspicuous member in the Petrograd Committee of Workmen's and Soldiers' Delegates, an able Parliamentarian and a convincing speaker. Prince Shakhovskoy had been Secretary of the Duma and at the time of his appointment to the Cabinet was Director of the Grain Elevators. The Food Controller—Pietchekhonoff—is a journalist who founded the People's Freedom Party, which, while adopting the programme of the Social Revolutionary Party, rejected terrorism as too excessive a means for achieving their ends.

On the re-organisation of the Ministry gloom gave way to gladness. The effect of the new concord was magnetic. The generals who had resigned withdrew their resignations and a conference between all the army heads and the government was held at Petrograd where plans were discussed for a vigorous offensive. The breath of life was infused into the forces at the front.

Even the Council of Workmen's and

GUTCHKOFF

MILYUKOFF

RODZIANKO

KONOVALOFF

Soldiers' Delegates rose to the occasion and issued a stirring appeal to the Army urging it to fight on to a peace dictated by victory alone. It declared:

"The workmen and peasants of Russia longed for peace, but it must be a general peace of all the nations and the result of their common agreement. A separate peace is an impossible thing, which must not be allowed to interfere with or embarrass the events of the world. It is evident that in this case German imperialism after having defeated our Western Allies, will turn against us the whole power of its arms, will seize our country and will enslave the Russian people."

Dominating the entire remade government, however, was the personality of Kerensky. He rose to this fresh occasion with all the splendid purpose and patriotism that had marked him in every other crisis. One of his first official acts was to visit the Congress of Peasant Delegates which had just convened in Petrograd, to whom he made a characteristically impassioned speech which sounded the vibrant note of reconstruction and order. He called upon the soldiers and sailors present to make a heroic effort for the country and he declared his intention to go to the front and talk to the men in the trenches. He received a great ovation.

He at once issued the following Order of the Day to the Army:

"The country is in danger and each one must do what he can to avert it. No request to be allowed to resign made in the desire to escape responsibility at a time so grave as the present will be accepted by me. Deserters are enjoined to return to the Army and the fleet within the time already specified, namely by May 28th. All infractions of these instructions will be severely punished."

The formation of the new Ministry solved the whole question of a Russian Constitution. The Duma surrendered its powers, remaining as a sort of watchdog of the nation's interests. The Council of Workmen's and Soldiers' Delegates assumed the dignity and dimension of a Parliament while the Provisional Government became the Executive. The threatened duality of authority vanished like a horrid dream.

The Provisional Government immediately

issued a declaration of its principles which embodied the following:

"In its foreign policy the Provisional Government, rejecting in concert with the entire people all thought of a separate peace, adopts openly as its aim the re-establishment of a general peace which shall not tend toward either domination over other nations or the seizure of their national possessions, or the violent usurpation of their territories—a peace without annexations or indemnities, and based on the rights of nations to decide their own affairs.

"In the firm conviction that the fall of the régime of Czardom in Russia and the consolidation of democratic principles in our internal and external policy will create in the Allied democracies new aspirations towards a stable peace and the brotherhood of nations, the Provisional Government will take steps towards bringing about an agreement with the Allies on the basis of its declaration of April 9th.

"Convinced that the defeat of Russia and her Allies would not only be a source of the greatest calamity to the people, but would postpone or make impossible the conclusion of a world-wide peace on the basis indicated above, the Provisional Government believes firmly that the Russian revolutionary army will not suffer the German troops to destroy our Western Allies and then throw themselves upon us with the full force of their arms."

Out of revolt had come reconstruction. The face of the nation was once more turned toward the light.

NO crisis has ever called to its standard a fitter company of captains than the men who made the Russian Revolution. They were the kind of volunteers that an American emergency might have recruited. Among them mingled millionaire and radical; soldier and dreamer; professor and proletariat. Strange company to be enlisted from the legions of Empire. There were Social and Constitutional Democrats; Middlegrounders and Conservatives—veterans who had survived the terror of Red Sunday, who had debated in cellars even as they now presided in palaces—patriots and warriors all who had staked life and fortune upon the Great Issue. You saw them and you realised that they were the keepers of democracy. You comprehended too that the Revolution had not been a one-man task but the product of an inspired team-work.

These men had been the bulwark of the dark hour of deliverance and they remained

the safeguard of its fruitage.   So long as
they survived you had no fear of the future.
As I saw them at work they reminded me of
the Board of Directors of a vast corporation. Vitality, vigour and vision were theirs
and the business they had begun to admin-
ister had a branch wherever men dwelt in
content or desired to be free.

They sat in the stately assembly room of
the Marie Palace where, by one of the many
ironies that marked the remaking of Russia,
the Old Council of Ministers had throttled
freedom through all the years of the nation's
servitude. Over them and flanking the superb white marble Florentine mantelpiece
hung life-size paintings of Alexander II and
Alexander III. In former times the semi-
circle of seats where the Ministers sat faced
a full length portrait of Nicholas the Deposed. That old group of servile courtiers
could look up at their royal master and be-
hold the bearded face which smiled upon the
deliberations that debased the nation. But
now that space where once hung the likeness
of the last of the Romanoffs to wear a crown,
was a virgin mass of white crêpe. The
Czar's picture had been blotted from sight

even as he himself had passed into eclipse.

In the session the Provisional Ministry unfolded a gallery worthy of a Carlyle portraiture. In the centre sat Lvoff, the zealot Prince who had become Premier, and at his right—typical of the new Russian democracy—was Kerensky the Firebrand—pale, eloquent, passionate. On his left was the white-haired Milyukoff, veteran of long wars of progress. Then, too, were the nimble-minded Tereshtchenko, the Sugar-beet King, who had left his own millions to rehabilitate the fortunes of his country; Gutchkoff, the banker soldier-of-fortune, who had fought from Tibet to South Africa and at whose behest the Czar signed the abdication that was the death warrant of his line; Konavoloff, who had turned from the unromantic textile manufacture to face machine guns in the streets; Shingareff, the onetime doctor, who was saving liberty instead of life, and all the rest. Only the massive Rodzianko was missing. The glory of a nation was written in their leadership. Whatever fate befall them in the days to come, their names will live in the stirring record of their times.

From the lips of these Washingtons, Hamiltons, Jeffersons and Lincolns of the Russian Revolution—(there were no Marats, Dantons or Robespierres)—I heard the epic tale of the Seven Days out of whose ordeal emerged the infant liberty.

Each of these men brought to his post a ripe experience; all had been tested in the fires of scorching ordeal and had not been found wanting. The career of the Premier is typical. Long before the Revolution, down-trodden Russia and more especially the peasant ground under the heel of autocracy knew him as friend, guide and philosopher. He was born in Moscow and early in life made a trip to the United States where he tramped over a large section of the middle and far west. Here he got his first draught of democracy and like a strong spirit it burned into his system.

In 1891 when the failure of the harvest brought the horrors of famine to millions of Russian homes, he acquired his first reputation as a philanthropist, for he strove with all the power and wealth at his command to feed the starving, and more especially the peculiarly oppressed government of

Tula.   Here he encountered the reactionary
influences of the old régime which sought to
prove as usual that all was well with the
people, that the pangs of hunger which cried
out for relief were really a state of mind.

It is in connection with the great Zemstvos Union, however, that Prince Lvoff made
his great reputation as a public benefactor.
The Zemstvos, as most people know, is a
public spirited organisation very much like
a City or County Council which has a
branch in nearly every community of any
consequence in Russia.   When the war with
Japan began, the Zemstvos immediately ex-
tended its field of operations to relieve the
sick and help the wounded soldiers.   During
this great national tragedy the Prince made
repeated visits to the front and by his inspiring presence and unfaltering effort, en-
deared himself not only to the host that bled
and died on those eastern fields, but to the
mothers, fathers, sisters and brothers who
were left behind to mourn and to suffer.

Prince Lvoff came into particular prominence in 1904 when Russia's dawn began.
He was one of the foremost among those
who petitioned the Emperor for reforms and

when the First Duma was wrested from a
grudging Government he was elected to represent the electors of Tula.　He at once
developed those qualities of initiative and
construction which have made him one of
Russia's foremost public servants.　His
long study of the agrarian problem together
with his familiarity with popular needs
equipped him for a very large service.

During the two months of that memorable
session he made various speeches pointing
out the errors of the old rule and urging
the need of a closer co-operation between
the government and the people.　Under his
inspiration the Assembly devoted itself seri-
ously to the question of food supply and one
of the results was the formation of a Food
Commission.　When the Duma adjourned
the Prince devoted himself exclusively to
the Zemstvos and Civic work.　Moscow
showed its tangible appreciation by electing
him a Municipal Councillor and member of
the Zemstvos for the Government of Moscow and subsequently by making him
Mayor.

At the beginning of the present war a
wave of popular confidence unanimously

placed him at the head of the All Russia Union of Zemstvos—the federation of all the local bodies—and from this time on he loomed large in national affairs.

The Union at once duplicated and then expanded its work of the Russo-Japanese conflict. It undertook the responsibility for providing food, clothing, medicine and sanitary equipment for the army, establishing a close working contact with the Red Cross and had an active part in providing for disabled soldiers upon their discharge from the hospitals. In this way thousands of battered human wrecks were rescued from becoming derelicts.

Over all this many-sided effort Prince Lvoff laid his masterful hand. One week saw him at the front ministering among the wounded, the next found him presiding at a Zemstvo Union, a model of suave and parliamentary perfection.

I like to remember my first sight of him. It was in the hideous yellow and white building misnamed a palace that stands just off the Nevsky sentinelled by the huge statue of Catherine the Great. Here, in the very lair of the reaction that was, I found this slight stooped, bearded little man, whose manner was kindly, almost too benevolent, and who met me with a grave but charming courtesy. You have but to look into his eyes to see the reflection of a great soul.

He sat at an elaborate desk littered with papers. By one of those many contrasts developed by the Revolution it was the very same desk from which Protopopoff issued the orders that gagged and bound Russia. On the walls of the ante-room just outside were the pictures of many of Lvoff's predecessors, some of them, like Pleve and Stolypin, who had paid with their lives for the power they wielded.

Like many Russians, Prince Lvoff is both emotional and eloquent. He is very likely to begin a conversation with a foreigner in French and when feeling stirs him and he kindles to his subject he lapses swiftly into Russian.

I remarked on the tide of time that had landed him in the seat of Sturmer and Protopopoff.

"Ah," he replied, and his eyes lighted up, "they were the slave drivers."

"And you?" I continued.

PRINCE GEORGE LVOFF

"We are the servants of the people," he answered. "Autocracy in Russia is dead forever."

In these last words the Prime Minister unconsciously interpreted himself for he has indeed been the servant of his nation.

The best-known member of the first Provisional Cabinet, so far as the outside world is concerned, is Paul Milyukoff. For twenty-five years he led the good fight. From youth to middle age and then beyond he carried with him not only an amazing vitality but also a sweet optimism and an abiding faith in the future. He lived to see that long dream realised and with such an outpouring of freedom that he was well compensated for the hardships he had suffered.

Although he was the one purely academic member of the original Revolutionary Government his career has been animated.

After his graduation from Moscow in 1886 he became a lecturer on Russian history but it was not long before he was deposed on the ground of being "politically unsound." His strong radical convictions made his presence in Russia undesirable so he took up his abode at Sofia where he lectured on general history at the University. In 1889 he was permitted to return to Russia where he engaged in literary and journalistic work. He started a magazine called *God's World,* and was soon after called upon to make the first of the many sacrifices that he made for conscience and freedom. One night he presided at a harmless assembly of students. The police, however, had different opinions. They regarded it as a "secret political conspiracy," Milyukoff was arrested and spent six months in prison.

In 1902 he went to America where he delivered a course of lectures on Russia at the University of Chicago. His forceful powers of expression and his intelligent grasp of democracy gained for him a large audience. Those were the years of research and he spent the greater part of 1904 and the beginning of 1905 in London working in the British Museum.

But the Voice of Revolution was calling to him from his native land. He returned to Petrograd with summer and devoted himself heart and soul to the liberation movement which was soon to be drenched in blood but which was to have its reward in the

"We are the servants of the people," he answered. "Autocracy in Russia is dead forever."

In these last words the Prime Minister unconsciously interpreted himself for he has indeed been the servant of his nation.

The best-known member of the first Provisional Cabinet, so far as the outside world is concerned, is Paul Milyukoff. For twenty-five years he led the good fight. From youth to middle age and then beyond he carried with him not only an amazing vitality but also a sweet optimism and an abiding faith in the future. He lived to see that long dream realised and with such an outpouring of freedom that he was well compensated for the hardships he had suffered.

Although he was the one purely academic member of the original Revolutionary Government his career has been animated.

After his graduation from Moscow in 1886 he became a lecturer on Russian history but it was not long before he was deposed on the ground of being "politically unsound." His strong radical convictions made his presence in Russia undesirable so he took up his abode at Sofia where he lectured on general history at the University. In 1889 he was permitted to return to Russia where he engaged in literary and journalistic work. He started a magazine called *God's World,* and was soon after called upon to make the first of the many sacrifices that he made for conscience and freedom. One night he presided at a harmless assembly of students. The police, however, had different opinions. They regarded it as a "secret political conspiracy," Milyukoff was arrested and spent six months in prison.

In 1902 he went to America where he delivered a course of lectures on Russia at the University of Chicago. His forceful powers of expression and his intelligent grasp of democracy gained for him a large audience. Those were the years of research and he spent the greater part of 1904 and the beginning of 1905 in London working in the British Museum.

But the Voice of Revolution was calling to him from his native land. He returned to Petrograd with summer and devoted himself heart and soul to the liberation movement which was soon to be drenched in blood but which was to have its reward in the

First Duma. Milyukoff was elected as a member of Petrograd. The Government, however, regarded him as too dangerous an element even to be trusted in those near halls of free discussion. So he remained on the outside and exerted a powerful influence. He helped to organise the Constitutional Democratic Party—the so-called Cadets— became their President and likewise the inspiration of the movement.

He alone among the forces that fought for freedom maintained the serene optimism which has guided and sustained him through all the troubled waters. After the hideous slaughter at Moscow he said to Henry W. Nevinson, an English author then in Petrograd:

"The reaction cannot last very long. The Moscow rising was a great mistake and at the end of it educated people and the well-to-do would be permanently set against change. But the Government's violence has kept them on our side. The 'classes' are as much sickened by the slaughter as other people. They have learnt that it is the Government and not the revolutionists who are the party of destruction and disorder. Reaction? Why, it is already over. The spirit of the thing is dead."

"The spirit of the thing" was not dead but the rot had started at the root and Milyukoff lived to see the foul structure totter. The years between the first Duma and the Revolution of 1917 were spent by him in unremitting public service. His tongue and his pen were geared incessantly to the freedom that struggled against such heavy odds. He served in the third and fourth Imperial Dumas and he found time amid all his distracting labours to found the *Retch,* now one of the leading Petrograd newspapers, and he made it the medium of fearless, brilliant and persistent attack on the old order. No other man in Russia had so conspicuous a part in laying bare the abuses and the excesses of reaction. Daily he put his head into the noose. How he escaped is a mystery. One of the chief contributory causes of the Revolution was his famous speech in the Duma in November, already referred to in this book, which laid bare the whole infamous pro-German conspiracy which was to debase Russia and deliver her into the hands of her enemies. With that speech, Milyukoff went to the very last limit to which a fearless and unconquerable patriotism could go.

It was on the Easter Sunday after the Revolution that I met Milyukoff. Fair skies and spring sunshine smiled on Petrograd; the city rang with the peal of joyous church bells. A freed people paraded the streets. Their proudest holiday finery was the badge of liberty. Winter had gone and the world seemed renewed and glad. But it was no gladder and no more renewed than this blue-eyed professor who saw in all happy awakening about him the realisation of his cherished ideals.

It was on that day he said to me:

"For many years the Russian people have consciously and unconsciously been preparing for liberty and democracy. Locally every Russian community has been self-governing and in the last analysis democracy simply means self-government. Now that the old oppression is forever gone and with it every symbol of suppression of free speech and free institutions, the country will go forward to a realisation of its great destiny which is a proud place among the democracies of the world.   And part of that larger destiny is brotherhood with America."

I saw Milyukoff many times after that first meeting, often when the fierce currents of discord and dissension swirled about him. He never lost his faith or his courage.   He was willing to put his very body into the breach, content if it only momentarily stopped the inrushing flood.

When for the sake of harmony and re-construction he surrendered his Cabinet post that the new freedom might live, he took his place in the ranks of democracy with the same high sense of service and loyalty that had dictated all his other sacrifices.   Courage, vision and stamina meet in Paul Mil-yukoff.   He is both fighter and dreamer.

Now turn to his co-patriot—Michael Rod-zianko, that mammoth of a man whose bulk rose like a mountain of refuge when the storm of Revolution broke.   Physically he would make half a dozen Lvoffs.   Just to look at him is to get an impression of strength and power.   He comes from a Cos-sack family and was born for the army.   Be-fore he was out of his teens he was in the

Imperial House Guards with which he served for many years with distinction.

For ten years, that is from 1886 to 1896, Rodzianko was Marshal of the Nobility of the district of Novomskovsk, preparing himself for the outstanding part which he was destined to play in the politics of his country. In 1902 he took his stand bravely with those who rallied to the October Manifesto, which was the birth certificate of the Duma. To these convictions he remained true throughout the vicissitudes of the first three Dumas. His loyalty was rewarded in 1912 when he was elected President of the Chamber.

Since the outbreak of war he has combined a lofty patriotism with unswerving devotion to his constitutional principles. In a notable utterance during the early days of the struggle and addressing himself to Russia's enemies, he said:—"You think dissension and dislike divide us, whereas all the peoples inhabiting the boundless lands of Russia are joined in one vast family since danger threatens our common country."

Rodzianko broods like a mighty spirit over the Duma. When he sits silent in the President's chair you can feel his very presence; when he talks the great Catherine Hall echoes as with the roar of a cataract. Yet this giant can be as tender as a child. I have seen him shaken by emotion that left him speechless. Rodzianko is a great deal more than President of the Duma; he is the vital force in the reconstruction of Russia who must be reckoned with whatever group attains the ascendency.

So, too, with Alexander Gutchkoff. Long before the dawn of the Revolution which gave him such prominence, he had been a conspicuous and picturesque figure in Russian liberal life.

No member of the Cabinet had had so varied or stirring a career. He had fought under half a dozen flags, a stormy petrel that flapped his wings in as many lands.

Gutchkoff was born in Moscow, the son of wealthy parents. After graduating from the University in his native place he devoted himself to the textile industry. His early ambition was for a parliamentary career, not through the Zemstvos, however, but by way of the Bourse Committee, the Congress of Commerce and Industry and other similar organisations. Possessed of ample means, he was able to gratify his desire for a public career, and he became a member of the Municipal Council of Moscow and worked on various commissions. Like Lvoff he laboured manfully to relieve the distress caused by the famine in 1891.

But all this was rather tame for a man whose instinct was action. When disorder started in unhappy Armenia and massacres began to horrify the world he was one of the first on the scene to offer his sword and his service. For a moment he turned to peaceful pursuit for he became Chief of Highways for the new railway which was started through Manchuria. Here, however, he got another taste of fighting, because he figured in more than one engagement against the wild native tribes. Tibet was still a forbidden land, so he went there in search of adventure, and when the Boer War started he promptly departed for South Africa and enlisted against the British. He fought for six months, when he was incapacitated and invalided home with a wound in his leg.

With the astounding versatility which has

marked his whole crowded lifetime he took up the threads of commerce again and became the Director of a Bank. But no sooner was he safely settled in his new work than the Revolution in Macedonia broke out and he became involved in the bloody maelstrom that swept the Balkans.

The Russo-Japanese war found Gutchkoff a ready and willing recruit. He became director of the Red Cross and conducted operations in the theatre of war itself. When the Russians retreated from Mukden he remained in the town with his surgeons in order to take care of the wounded and was captured by the Japanese and kept a prisoner until the end of the war. He returned to Russia in time to find the Revolutionary movement of 1905 in full swing and he promptly joined it.

When "the Union of October Seventeenth" was founded as a political party, he was chosen as its President, and took a lively part in the political struggle of the parties before the election of the first Duma. The victory of the party of Cadets made it impossible for him to enter the First and Second Imperial Duma. But he did not lay down his

arms for in Moscow he founded the paper
The Voice of Moscow, and continued the
fight. In 1907 he was elected a member of
the Third Duma. Preferring the Duma to
the Imperial Council, he appeared as leader
of the party of Octobrists, and in 1910 was
elected President of the Duma after the resignation of Khomyakoff.

In the summer, however, he fought a duel
with Urusoff and was sentenced to prison,
which necessitated his resignation as Chief
Executive of the parliament. When he was
released his colleagues welcomed him with a
re-election to the Presidency, which he again
resigned in 1911.

Gutchkoff was the first to denounce the
espionage of Myasojedoff and when the latter, assuming the pose of outraged virtue,
challenged his enemy to a duel, he was at
once accepted. He was like a child in Gutchkoff's hands.

No man in Russia realised more keenly the
inefficiencies of the nation's war machine
than Gutchkoff. His first disillusionising
contact with it had been in the war with
Japan, and in the years that followed he saw
the slow disintegration of military organisa-

tion. When the Great War crashed into civilisation he shuddered for the welfare of his country. Like thousands of his country-men, he beheld with humiliation the criminal inadequacy and inefficiency of transport and supplies. It was largely due to his efforts that the War Industries Committee was formed. He became President of its Cen-tral Committee, and aided in no small way to develop the great aid that this body brought to the national defence.

You have already seen in the narrative of the Revolution how Gutchkoff figured in every great crisis of that series of crises. None of them greater, however, or more sig-nificant than the historic moment when he dictated the abdication of the Czar. When the Provisional Ministry was being fash-ioned, his was the only name mentioned for the Portfolio of War and Marine. When he took the post a real warrior was on the job. His impatience led him to resign when the integrity of the new government was menaced by the Socialistic demagogues, and this unfortunate retirement prevented him from rendering an administration that would have undoubtedly been brilliant and effective.

The extraordinary variety of achievement and experience which characterised the members of the First Provisional Government is expressed in Michael Tereshtchenko, the Child of the Cabinet, for he is only thirty-three years old. Here you have a man whose career ranges all the way from professional pianist to Minister of Finance. It has been a marvel of efficiency.

Tereshtchenko is the son of a peasant who became the Sugar-beet king of Southern Russia. He inherited this title and with it an income of several million roubles a year. He was educated at Warsaw and Petrograd and then studied music, for which he had a great natural aptitude, at Leipzig. His experience in Germany gave him a disinclination for trade, so he became a co-director of the famous Marinsky Theatre in Petrograd, where he often played the piano in public. On the death of his father, however, he was forced to take up the control of the immense business to which he had succeeded, but he never permitted himself to be completely immersed in commerce.

But when the war came he gave himself up to the struggle. Like various other rich

young men he organised a sanitary squad
(for the hygienic work in the army was sadly
inadequate) and he worked in the trenches
and hospitals with his men like an ordinary
private. He financed several Red Cross hospitals. All the while the realisation of the
incompetency of the national munition organisation jarred on him. He found a kindred spirit in Gutchkoff and under the latter's guidance helped to organise the now
famous War Industry Committee. Tereshtchenko insisted that the workmen be given a
representative on it. The wisdom of this
step was at once proved by an increased output for it brought harmony and good-will.

This then was the type of man who was
called upon to become Steward of Russia's
bankrupt treasury. Most men would have
shrunk from the peculiar hardship of a task
which involved the complete rehabilitation of
the nation. His business training came into
good stead, for he organised a complete system of bookkeeping, and for the first time the
Russian Government found out precisely
where its accounts stood. It was Tereshtchenko who conceived and launched the

MICHAEL TERESHTCHENKO

Loan of Liberty.   He wrote every line of advertising that was put out.

He is the one man who gives you the immediate impression of swift and dynamic American business methods.   If he lived in the United States he would be called a hustler.   Shut your eyes as he talks to you and you think you are listening to a well-bred Englishman who has spent all his life at Oxford. His English is flawless. He even has an English accent.   He is live, sinuous, active, yet with the face and eye of a poet.   Tereshtchenko is proudly and passionately Russian, and he sees in the awakened nation a New Nationalism that will create new ideals of character and achievement.

Full mate to Tereshtchenko in vigour and vim is Alexander Konavoloff, the textile manufacturer, who, like so many of his colleagues, found time in the midst of a busy business life to devote himself to the public good.   He had a very intimate connection with the organisation of the War Industry Committee, and was vice-President of the Central Committee.   When Gutchkoff was compelled to retire for a time on account of illness he directed the entire work of the organisation.

He was a member of the Fourth Duma from the Government of Kostroma. Here he immediately asserted himself as a man of force and distinction and was made vice-President of the Committee of Commerce and Industry. His forty-one years rest very lightly on his shoulders for like his colleague in the Finance post he is virile and active— an inspired man for his post. I can sum up his qualities in no better way than to repeat what one of Russia's ablest business men said to me shortly before I left Petrograd.

"Konavoloff has made the dullest department of the government the liveliest."

In Andrew Shingareff the constructive traditions of the men in the Ministry are admirably maintained. He is a doctor who left a successful practice to join the many patriots who subordinated personal interest to the national welfare. He graduated in medicine from the University of Moscow and began his public work as a physician in the Government of Voronesh, founding a village hospital in the village of Bolshaya Vereika. Later he practised medicine in the Zemstvo of Voronesh and managed the sanitary department of the Zemstvo Administration of Voronesh, taking part also in the work of the Government Committee on the Needs of the Rural Industry. At the same time he took part as member in the Zemstvo meetings of the Umansky district and the Government of Tambov. During the revolutionary movement of 1905 he joined the Union of Liberation and became the editor of *Voroneshskoe Slovo*. The Government of Voronesh elected him for the Duma, where he made effective speeches on the many important legislative projects and worked on the budget and territorial commission.

You get an index to the character of Alexander Manuiloff when you find out what he said when he assumed the post of Minister of Public Education. He was discussing his work with some friends when he declared: "If I can have my way, every child in Russia, no matter where he is born, will have a common school education. I consider this the most important part of my work."

This man, formerly a professor in the University of Moscow, is a famous economist whose works are known not only in Russia but throughout the world. One of his best works was his thesis for a Master's degree on "The Irish Land Leases." Manuiloff showed his protest against bureaucratic methods by resigning his professorship at the University of Moscow when Kasso became Minister of Public Instruction. He became content with a post in the minor University of Shanyavsky until the advent of freedom, when he came into his own again.

That the New Russia is determined to entrust her larger national tasks to specialists was evidenced in the appointment of Nicholas Nekrasoff to the Ministry of Ways and Communications. Under the old order this post was almost invariably filled by some bureaucrat whose chief qualifications were either acquiescence to the corruption that fairly dripped about him, or influence with the Government. Nekrasoff, however, is a trained and experienced engineer who, after graduating from the School of Engineers in Petrograd taught for a considerable time at the Technological Institute at Tomsk. After studying abroad he returned to become a special professor of Buildings and Bridges. He was also a member of the Advisory Commission of the Department of Building and Construction in the University town where he lived.

During the student disturbances at Tomsk he came forward as a valiant champion of the principles of academic autonomy and from this time until the Revolutionary outbreak of 1905 he was in the forefront of the battle for free speech and freer action. He organised the Yalta section of the Constitutional Democratic Party, served in the Third and Fourth Dumas from Tomsk where he made his presence felt. Nekrasoff is only thirty-five years old and a fine type of a vigorous, open-minded, up-standing democracy that was the salvation of Russia.

Like Shingareff, Russia's State Controller, Ivan Godneff was a doctor who quit a lucrative practice to work for the public good. As member of the Zemstvos of the district and government of Kazan and the Duma he worked on many Zemstvos and city commissions; he studied city and territorial affairs in detail and was permanent president of the Revision Commission. In Kazan, Godneff was President of the Orphan's Court, member of the Government Department on Territorial affairs, honourary trustee of a school and member of the Board of Trustees of the Marie High School. At the same time he did not sever his connection with the Caucasian University where he had a great reputation as lecturer. His eloquent tongue joined with Milyukoff's in exposing the injustice and iniquity of the old order.

The average Anglo-Saxon associates the office of Over Procurator of the Holy Synod with a senile and bewhiskered gentleman stiff with the brocaded vestments of the Church. Vladimir Lvoff is no such person, for he is an enterprising revolutionist, a leader in the Octobrist party and an editor of force and power. He has been a prop of the Zemstvos and a factor in the Duma.

That touch of exile, tinged with romance, which is part of the equipment of most prominent Russian Revolutionists, is revealed to a remarkable degree in Theodore Rodicheff, who became Minister of Finnish Affairs in the First Provisional Cabinet. In variety and adventure his career rivals that of Gutchkoff.

After graduating in law from the University of Petrograd, he enlisted with the Southern Serbs in their fight for freedom against the Turks. He came through this campaign unscathed, and on his return to Russia was made Marshal of Nobility of the district of Vesyegonsk, where he served for twelve years. In 1894 he first ran afoul of the Government when on behalf of the Union of Tver he sent an address to the Emperor pleading for a Constitution for the Russian nation. This was of course the highest treason and he was severely punished. One penalty that he had to pay was a complete deprivation of the right to take part in any public meeting. Despite this ban his colleagues in the Zemstvo of Tver elected him President of their body. Thus he still had a field for his patriotism and his energy.

Rodicheff felt, however, that Petrograd was his field so he settled down there as a barrister in 1900. The very next year he was exiled from the capital because he signed the well-known protest against the killing of the students. In 1904, however, all his rights were restored to him and he was therefore on the ground when the revolutionary movement began.   He was one of the organisers of the Constitutional Democratic Party and henceforth had conspicuous part in the great movement for the uplift and the emancipation of his people.   He has the peculiar distinction of having served in all four Imperial Dumas.

Such is the fibre of the men who made the Revolution and then led the Reconstruction. Yet they are only part of that larger and unsung array, both in and out the Duma, that kept the faith through all the years of oppression.   They are likewise the Hope of To-morrow.

THE Russian Revolution produced a democracy, but it also revealed the rarest of human institutions—a great leader. A week before the first shot was fired that made a bonfire of the old Russian system, Alexander Kerensky was scarcely known outside the circles of the Labour party in Petrograd; when the tumult and the shouting had ceased his name was on every tongue, and before a month had passed he was part of Russia's prayers. History records no rise so swift or so sensational. This man's achievement makes him the one distinct and outstanding personality of the whole crowded epoch.

In Kerensky Russian democracy gives illuminating demonstration of every fundamental principle for which democracy stands. He interprets the new order in brilliant and convincing fashion. Here was a poor and practically obscure young man—he was barely thirty-five when he came into his great prominence—who in a single week assumed the role of national saviour and made himself the Lloyd George of his country.

So rapid was his rise to fame that the human interest historians had difficulty in placing him. Kerensky was born in Simbirsk, where his father was Principal of the local High School. He received his first instruction at Tashkent, where he completed the high school course, after which he studied law at the University of Petrograd. He could not afford to embark at once upon the uncertain sea of a new legal practice, so he became assistant to a Commissioner of Oaths and subsequently became one of these officials himself.

While at school Kerensky was known for his ready speech and fervid oratory, which let loose at the slightest provocation. When he finally took up his law practice in Petrograd he immediately allied himself with the Labour Party, and at once made his presence felt. In his practice he specialised in political cases and on more than one occasion defended his clients with such impassioned force and with such unrestrained condemnation of reactionary methods that he narrowly escaped prosecution himself. Despite his reputation for more or less irresponsible decla-ation, he showed real strength of character and when this quality was put to the test at the supreme crisis of his life, it stood revealed as pure gold. His attitude in the Fourth Duma, to which he was elected from the Government of Saratoff, heightened the impression that perhaps after all this young spreadeagle orator who had a speech for every occasion, was something of a man after all.

Such was the brief and unadorned approach to that great hour when Kerensky was to stand disclosed as the real Republic Maker. His close contact and association with the revolutionary workmen groups enabled him to keep in close touch with everything that was transpiring during these momentous weeks in February and early March when hunger, irritation and the long smouldering protest against the iron despotism were slowly but surely bringing revolt to a head. Although he was a member of the Duma, his real interest and association—born of every bond of birth and conviction—was with the Extremists. When revolution broke, he found himself in a curiously anom-

alous situation. The conservatism of the
Duma claimed his loyalty, while on the other
hand the fierce and unrestrained radicalism
of the Socialists and their allies in the Council of Workmen's and Soldiers' Delegates
appealed to his fervour and his imagination.
Never was a man so beset. He might have
allied himself with the Reds, become their
flaming leader and gone straight to the Presidency of the rampant republic they were
proclaiming.

It was then that Kerensky cast his lot with
Reason and with that great decision—it was
merely part of his destiny—he became Russia's Handy Man. With his colleague,
Cheidze, he formed the link between the Radicals and the Duma during the days when dissension and discord threatened the very life
of the new freedom. He dominated every
situation; faced all the crises that crowded
so thick and fast.

How Kerensky survived those weeks was
a miracle. His none too robust constitution
was subjected to a well-nigh incredible strain.
Day and night he was in almost continuous
conference—pleading, debating, arguing.
When he rose to speak in the public assem-

blies he was the target of bitter verbal attack; when he went forth into the streets his life was in constant danger. He lived on his nerves and his indomitable will kept him going.

By what process did he achieve this compelling triumph over all obstacles? In the answer is his first kinship with Lloyd George. It lies in an oratory that is perhaps his greatest gift. Like the wizard Welshman who has stood so often in Britain's breach, he speaks with an emotion that becomes a sweeping flood of passion. He lacks the Lloyd George brilliancy of imagery and he has none of that poetry and vision which are the birthright of "England's Darling." But he has a personal appeal that is well-nigh irresistible. It is convincing because it is sincere.

Linked with this sincerity is an iron courage. During the whole period of riotous upheaval when the new Government was shaping and when Petrograd, intoxicated with its new freedom, had swung from one extreme to another, he risked everything for his convictions. He bearded his defiers whatever the cost. When his old colleagues now en-

throned in the Council of Workmen's and
Soldiers' Delegates accused him of disloy-
alty he went straight to their midst and defended himself.

With that fine sense of the dramatic which
he shares with Lloyd George, he suddenly
appeared in the Assembly Chamber. His
coming had been unheralded and unannounced. As he entered the room his name
had just been uttered with derision and almost contempt by one of his socialistic crit-
ics. He strode swiftly down the aisle to the
rostrum and faced the crowd. Instantly
there was a silence. His pallid face was
whiter than usual; his eyes flashed with fire.
He looked about him for a moment and then
began what was in many respects one of his
greatest speeches. Certainly it was one of
his most characteristic. This is what he said:

"Comrades, Soldiers and Officers!

"I have not had time to visit the representatives
of the society to which I belong. I have been
occupied the whole time with work which could
not be delayed, and this is what I have come to
say to you to-day.

"Up to this time there have been no misunder-
standings between us, but now I hear that people

are appearing among us who, spreading foolish rumours, wish to sow the seed of discord among the democratic masses.

"Five years from this chair I fought against the old régime, and accused it without ceasing. And I know the enemies of the people, I know how to deal with them. Until I became a member of the Duma I long found myself in the torture-chamber of Russian justice, and many of those who are fighting for freedom passed through my hands.

"During the war I have already advocated in secret sessions the changing of the 'Military Law,' the abolition of saluting and the improvement of the soldier's lot. (Loud cheers.)

"I became a member of the Duma that I might fearlessly tell how the Russian people enjoyed no rights and were oppressed by the old régime. As a representative of the democratic masses, I have done my duty till now without violating the general rights of man. I have always advocated them until I was almost tired of doing so, and now I am again before you at this Tribune, Comrades, and in my hands is all the power of the Russian Procurator General, and know that no one can be released from arrest without my consent.

"I have heard that rumours have been active among you to the effect that I am beginning to weaken in my attitude towards the old Government and to the Czar's family. I have heard that people have come among you who dare to

mistrust me. I warn all that I will not permit the
man who says this to show distrust of me, and
in my person to insult the Russian democracy.
I ask you either to exclude me from your midst
or to place your implicit trust in me.   (Loud
cheers and Bravo.)

"You are accusing the Provisional Government
and myself in that we are weakening in our attitude to the members of the Czar's family, that
we are leaving them in freedom and act conde-
scendingly towards them.

"But I would have you know that I have been
in Tsarskoe Selo, where I had an interview with
the Commandant of the Garrison, and spoke with
the soldiers. The Commandant of the Palace at
Tsarskoe Selo is a well known friend of mine,
and I trust him fully. The Garrison promised to
fulfil my orders only. All that takes place in
Tsarskoe Selo occurs with my knowledge.

"You appear to have entertained doubts that
certain members of the Czar's family have remained at large, but those alone are free who, together with you, protested against the old régime,
and the arbitrary rules of the Czardom. Dmitry
Pavlovich is free as he opposed the old Government to the end. He it was who engineered the
conspiracy and killed Rasputin. And he has full
right to remain as an ordinary officer in the ranks
of the Russian Army in Persia.

"I have set at liberty General Ivanoff, but he is
always under my surveillance in his private apartments. I have freed him because he is ill and old

and the doctors affirm that he would not live even three days if he remained in the surroundings in which he was placed.

"Comrades, Soldiers and Officers! Remember that the task of the Provisional Government is a great and responsible one.

"The Provisional Government stands for freedom, right and Russian independence, and will continue to do so until the end. On all of us, on our Provisional Government lies the single responsibility for the fate of our country, and in the name of our duty before the whole country we must all work in unity together.

"I will not go away from this Tribune until I have satisfied myself that there will be no other organisation save that of a democratic republic. (Extraordinary demonstration of enthusiasm.)

"Comrades, soldiers, there is now no army in the whole world so free as the Russian Army. You are free citizens, you have the right to form organisations, and this you have achieved in three days.

"To-morrow is the 27th of March. A whole month has passed from the moment when I greeted the first detachment of revolutionary troops who had come to the Tavritchesky Palace to place themselves at the disposal of the Provisional Government, and placed a guard of honour.

"I became a member of the Provisional Government as your representative, and your interests and views I will maintain as long as I have strength. The Provisional Government is listening to what you say. I should like you to know that in a few days' time a document will appear in which declaration will be made that Russia disclaims all the aims of military aggression.

"I am working for your welfare, so long as I retain your trust and so long as all are frank with me. But people have appeared who desire to sow the seeds of disunion among us. Remember, that in the name of national duty we must all work together, and if you wish, I will work with you; if you wish otherwise—I will go away. I want to know, do you believe in me or Not!! (Tremendous sensation and applause and universal cries expressing confidence.)

"I have come here not to justify myself and not to excuse myself before you. I only wished to say that I will not permit myself and the whole democracy of Russia to be held under suspicion! (Great ovation.)"

In this speech the real Kerensky stood revealed with all the intrepidity of soul that is his heritage. Such an effort could only have one finale—a superb ovation that literally swept the speaker off his feet. After that speech all criticism of Kerensky ceased and henceforth his leadership was implicitly—almost blindly, followed.

Kerensky has all of Lloyd George's genius of being able to sound out the populace and to find out what it wants. Like his Welsh colleague he makes every speech seem to be a direct and personal appeal to every individual in his audience. It is one of the master elements in the formula of successful popular oratory.

Scarcely had the Revolution subsided before Kerensky visited the front and asked the soldiers in the trenches to stand by the new order. He also made a flying trip to Helsingfors, the capital of Finland, and made an eloquent address to the Finnish Parliament. He made this trip with characteristic swiftness, so swift in fact that he did not even have a passport and was arrested on the Russian frontier. He got through, however. Unannounced he rose in the Chamber and claimed the privileges of the floor, saying:

"I am Kerensky, the new Minister of Justice, and I want to talk to you about the new government."

In similar abrupt fashion he made descent one day upon a sewing circle composed of fashionable women doing Red Cross work. Almost before they had time to wonder who or what he was he said:

"I am Kerensky the Red. Don't be
alarmed. I won't bite you. I merely came
here to tell you that we Radicals are not as
red as we are painted. When you go home
you can tell your family and friends that the
new government seeks no man's life. All it
wants is intelligent co-operation from everybody."

Thus Kerensky went his way placating the
unruly, harmonising the discordant—a tower
of strength to the new order. It was his overwhelming appeal that swung the Socialists
in line with the Provisional Government and
made the Coalition Cabinet possible: his
vivid personality swept the troops back to
discipline and defiance of the enemy.

In this pregnant moment of accord which
really saved the democracy he again demon-
strated the astounding parallel of Lloyd
George. He stepped from the Ministry of
Justice into the Portfolio of War and began
what will probably become a progressive
journey towards the Premiership.

If up to this time any man had questioned
the bigness of Kerensky his sacrifice now removed all doubt. Kerensky was a Socialist
and therefore an anti-imperialist. Yet in a

moment when he felt that his country needed a great sacrifice he met the emergency. No contrast in his life of contrasts was sharper. It was even more pronounced than the spectacle of Lloyd George, the one-time pro-Boer and Pacifist, sitting in the seat of Kitchener.

Shortly after he became Minister of War Kerensky made one of the many dramatic and intimate illuminations of his character. The whole country was aquiver with curiosity as to the policy of the Socialist Warrior. He lost no time in making his creed known. A congress of peasants had just convened in Petrograd. These were his own people, and to them he made his first declaration of the new principles, and with all the fire and passion at his command:

"Soldiers, Sailors and Officers," he said. "I call upon you to make a last heroic effort. I am your servant. Help me to show the world that the Russian army is not a demolished temple, but that it is strong and formidable, capable of making itself respected and of defending the free Republic of democratic Russia. It may appear strange that I, a civilian, who was never a soldier, have undertaken the heavy task of restoring discipline in the army, but I have accepted it because I understand that this discipline is based on honour, duty and reciprocal respect.

"I have never known what this discipline is, but nevertheless I propose to introduce an iron discipline into the army, and I am sure that I shall succeed. This discipline is necessary not only at the front but also in the interior of the country, in order to bring the liberty which has been conquered into the Constituent Assembly.

"I am shortly going to the front. Allow me, therefore, to say in the trenches that the Russian peasants wish to have the land which belongs to them, and that no force shall take it from them, but also allow me to say that the peasants demand that in order to achieve this object every one shall do his duty in a spirit of self-sacrifice."

Petrograd was still ringing with the cheers that followed this outburst when Kerensky issued his famous first Order of the Day to the Russian Army. It rang with the clarion call to duty and action.

I met Kerensky under circumstances that, had they been staged for the occasion, could not more fittingly present the character of

the man and the immense part he was play-
ing in the drama of Russian liberty. He had
hardly acclimated himself to the ministerial
atmosphere when I called on him at his office
in the Ministry of Justice. The appointment
was for ten o'clock in the morning and I arrived there a few moments before that time.

The crowd in the ante-room indicated that
I was at a Tribune of the people, because the
throng that filled nearly all the available
space represented the democracy of the hour.
Generals emblazoned with orders rubbed
shoulders with unwashed privates. You saw
merchant and washerwoman—priest and
atheist, uplifter and radical—all part of the
procession that had come to the cabinet of
a Father Confessor.

Sharply at ten o'clock the door opened, a
pale face peered out, bowed, smiled and then
withdrew. Kerensky was sizing up his audience. An attendant then appeared and es-
corted ten private soldiers into the inner
chamber. After an interval of ten minutes
they emerged and went their way. My time
had arrived, for an officer—one of the two
who were in constant attendance upon the
Minister, for he is the only member of the

Government who had an armed guard—appeared and asked me to enter.

I followed him and found myself in a small bare room. There was not a picture on the walls. But the moment I entered I felt that the place was vibrant with a definite presence. That presence was incarnated in the spare, almost ascetic figure of a man who sat at a plain, flat-topped desk fingering some papers. It was Kerensky at last. As I appeared he rose and came forward with his hand outstretched, saying:

"I am very sorry to have kept you waiting but I had to see a delegation of soldiers from the front. They came to me straight from the trenches, and they wanted to tell me their troubles immediately. I hope you didn't mind."

It was done with genuine charm and with a wistfulness too that was very captivating. I saw at once how and why Kerensky had succeeded with his fellowmen. He was very human.

He sat down and talked in a steady stream for an hour. Only Roosevelt surpasses him in ceaseless flow of speech. He talks as he has lived—earnestly, passionately, completely. Every effort he makes is a sap at his vitality. He fairly drains the well-springs of his life.

But more impressive than his speech is the appearance of the man. His face is white almost to ghastliness; his cheeks are gaunt; his eyes are deep, black, lustrous; he looks like one who has suffered and struggled and borne the great burdens. He incarnates the stuff of which martyrs are made.

We talked of many things that April day —of war, peace, democracy, the whole chaos into which the world seemed plunged. He displayed an amazing knowledge of affairs and I was not surprised to find that his two admirations were Lloyd George and Lincoln. Consciously he has made the lives of these two great leaders the models for his own. Unconsciously he has become, so far as his public career is concerned, the prototype of the first. Who knows but what he may not share with the great American Emancipator the glory of a kindred martyrdom!

No man who has watched Russia in the perilous days of her transition can question the fact that much of the future of the nation lies in the hollow of Kerensky's hand. Up to him was placed squarely the task of instilling into millions of simple, honest, illiterate and childlike people, the message of democracy. No other man in the country could attempt it with any hope of success. What he can do remains to be seen.

But one thing is certain. So long as Kerensky lives, so long will reason rule. The man who was the Cement of the Revolution will remain the Rock of Reconstruction.

XI—*The New Russia*

THROUGH the preceding pages has passed the panorama of the most remarkable popular upheaval since the French Revolution. It was achieved with a swiftness and a bloodlessness without parallel. The most patient and long suffering of all nations threw off the yoke of tyranny almost overnight. Never was retribution swifter and yet less terrible. A people who could show restraint when a long and poignant past cried out for vengeance are capable of still greater things.

The world that sat spellbound at the spectacle of a freed Russia forgot in the wonder of the moment that the Slav passion for liberty is no new thing. It had beat for decades against the bars of oppression. Siberia was merely one chapter in a tragic biography of protest written in blood and agony. What years of organised assassination tempered by the highest sacrifice could not achieve, was made possible by the Great War.

Save for the Kaiser-ridden domain where the Mailed Fist still clutched at the throat of popular will, the whole world desired Russian liberation. The one flaw in the otherwise perfect enactment of Russian deliverance was that it came at an untimely hour. It raised issues which will complicate and may neutralise the fruits of victory.

On the other hand, emancipation was only possible during the war. Without its superb stimulus the people could not have risen. The immense conflict welded the soul of Russia. It made the populace intolerant of the human rubbish that blocked the way of the national desire; it made the army their ally; it recreated the Cossack into a human being. One great lesson of the Revolution is that this war is the Supreme Revealer and not the least of its revelations is the light that pointed the path to Russian Democracy.

With a dispassionate review of all that has happened in Russia must come a larger understanding of the indiscretions that impeded reconstruction. Civilisation was somewhat led astray by the almost incredible calm and rapidity with which the revolt was carried out. Most people forgot that it was a complete revolution and not a mere change in Government. The whole structure of national organisation was uprooted. It was impossible to take a ready-made system off the shelf and substitute it for the hideous régime that had gone to its doom. Hence the disorder and the disunion; hence, too, the colossal problems that confront the New Russia.

More than one sober-minded man in Russia believed with Milyukoff that a Constitutional Monarchy was the first logical step toward a complete popular Government. The quick reaction that followed the sudden freedom, however, swung the huge body of sentiment around to the other extreme and the Moderates bowed to the Extremists. A Republic had to succeed the most buttressed of all autocracies—and at once.

Vast difficulties stand in the way of the realisation of this ideal. One hundred and eighty millions of people, many of them illiterate and most of them still imbued with the idea that their Chief Executive is a sort of god-head and entrusted with rulership for life, must be taught the fundamentals of democracy. Every one, male and female, has a vote. A mighty weapon has been fashioned that may become the bulwark of the new liberty or its undoing.

I know no better way of summing up this situation than to reproduce what Milyukoff said to me the last time I saw him. He was still in the Cabinet, and we stood at a window of the Foreign Office looking out on the immense square below. Across was the Winter Palace, red as the wrath that had enveloped it, but no redder than the flag of Revolution that floated from its roof.

"Russia will have a republic," he said. "It will be formally determined at a Constituent Assembly to be held as soon as possible. In the United States it would be a very easy matter to call and hold such a convention. But in Russia it is not so easy. The procedure is necessarily slow because so many obstacles lie in the path.

"First among these difficulties is the purely technical detail. Unlike America, Russia has no periodical census. Our statistics of population are therefore out of date. The great masses of Russian people must be prepared for universal suffrage and for a clear comprehension of popular representation of

THE AUTHOR'S PASSPORT (FRONT)

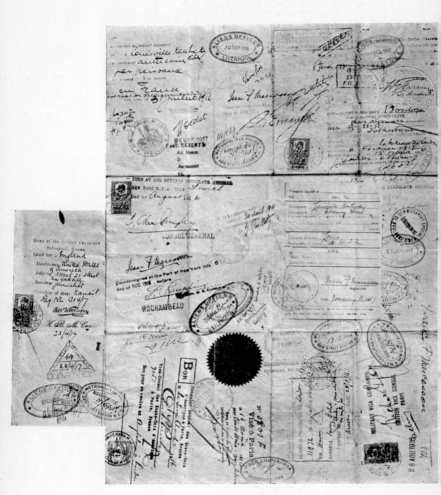

THE AUTHOR'S PASSPORT (REVERSE)

all kinds. To this end a Committee has been appointed to create a detailed programme for electing delegates to the convention which will doubtless be on a basis of one delegate to every large unit of population—perhaps one for every hundred thousand.

"The second difficulty in the way of an immediate calling up of a convention is military operation. Russia does not forget even in the midst of her new-found freedom that one permanent bulwark of that freedom is in a peace dictated by complete victory over the common enemy. The crisis on our fronts must be met and vanquished and this requires concentration of energy and resource.

"Personally I am not in favour of a United States of Russia, composed of national units like the Republic of Lithuania or the Republic of the Tartars. I believe in one great democratic State—a Brotherhood of territorial units each one capable of making its own by-laws but administered by officials named by the National Government. In this plan you would have an effective example of decentralisation which would avoid the inevitable conflict that would separate national entities each preserving its own integrity of race and speech.

"The salvation of popular government in the newest democracy lies in the preservation of National Unity."

Some of the ancient wrongs will not wait for formal parliamentary adjudication. Even before I left Russia, unrest had descended upon the peasantry and the storm began to break about the eternal agrarian question. As the idea of acquired freedom began to soak into the consciousness of the Russian agriculturist it brought a sudden understanding that at last all land was to be distributed equally. Save in a few isolated cases there was no actual pillage, but scores of estates have already been seized and the adjustment of the whole distribution problem will be one of the many problems that the reconstructed government will be called upon to solve.

A touch of sentiment may help to soften the herculean task of Russian reorganisation. It grew out of America's entry into the war. The effect of this historic event was almost indescribable. It thrilled the heart of a nation already tender with rejoicing and gave the war a sense of kinship and comfort.

President Wilson's reference to the Revolution in his memorable speech to Congress arraigning the Germans and arraying America on the side of World Humanity found grateful echo. I heard men like Prince Lvoff say:

"It is more than a coincidence that Russia's dawn of freedom and America's entry into the war for liberty should have happened at the same time. It was an Act of Providence."

The visit of the mission headed by Elihu Root came at a psychological moment. It found the new democracy a prey to unrest, verging for a moment upon disintegration. The calm and judicious exhortation of the great New York lawyer checked the flood of near-anarchy that for the moment threatened the impending republic. The mission not only strengthened the bonds between the two nations but opened up avenues of commercial relationship which in the end will forge the larger international link.

The rebirth of Russia, unlike the advent of the New France in the eighteenth century, will be unhampered by Royalist plot or by the opposition of a united monarchical Europe. It worked in a different way its miracles to perform. Out of the fateful Seven Days came the solemn warning to the Master of Potsdam that the day of the despot was done. The Russian upheaval leaves one remaining autocrat. Will the Kaiser follow his Royal cousin into the dusk?

Whatever happens in Russia—and no man can foresee the end—the Revolution kindled an unquenchable beacon on the mountain top of the century. It proclaims the flaming truth that government by, of, and for the people has at last arisen in a once benighted land.

Russia is mistress of her destiny.

Finished

THE END

J. H. Aug 29/17.

A. J. H. Sept. 14/17.